THE ART OF WEED BUTTER

A Step-by-Step Guide to Becoming a Cannabutter Master

MENNLAY GOLOKEH AGGREY

ULYSSES PRESS

Published by:
ULYSSES PRESS
P.O. Box 3440
Berkeley, CA 94703
www.ulyssespress.com

ISBN: 978-1-61243-872-6
Library of Congress Control Number: 2018959335

Printed in the United States by Sheridan Books Minnesota

10 9 8 7 6 5 4

Acquisitions editor: Casie Vogel
Managing editor: Claire Chun
Editor: Shayna Keyles
Proofreader: Renee Rutledge
Front cover design: David Hastings
Interior design and production: what!design @ whatweb.com
Photographs: © Sandra Blow except © Jake Lindeman front cover, back cover (middle), and on
    pages 6, 10, 12, 17, 25 26, 28, 32, 34 (right), 51 (top), 52; © Natasha Breen/shutterstock.com
    on page 37

For the matriarchy in the Aggrey family and the women in weed who have raised me. For Vivian Aggrey, for Leethia, for Jaynell, for Johnna, for Dierdre, and for the earth we live on.

May we steward the land and continue to grow the plants and cook the food that heals us.

CONTENTS

PREFACE

My name is Mennlay Golokeh Aggrey—a mouthful, right? I'm not a fancy chef, just a simple home cook with 13 years of experience as a professional in the legal cannabis industry. It was inevitable for me to begin infusing weed into some of my favorite everyday meals. And this harmonious marriage of the two has been so beneficial in my life that I want to share my journey with you.

I've grown a considerable amount of cannabis in my life and bushels upon bushels of my own food. These practices have given me a good glimpse into the process of what it takes to bring food to the table, and weed into a joint. It has given me a deep gratitude for this line of work and the strong belief that access to fresh food and cannabis is not only naturally healing, but a crucial human right.

My Journey

My affair with cannabis began in my youth, when I was suffering from a lot of depression. I was living away from home at a boarding school established to help intelligent kids from low-income families achieve. Weed was my first boyfriend, and in the face of the stereotypes, it kept me from drinking and doing drugs. What I found in cannabis was a vehicle to get outside of my head and into enjoying the abundant gift of my young life.

In 2005, work and weed first intersected when a long-distance college romance brought me to Humboldt County, California. Five hours north of San Francisco, this county dwells at the tip of Northern California. Home to a misty, foggy coast outlined by redwood trees, some of the oldest trees on our planet, I nestled into my first home as an adult—a small cottage with a fireplace, and an outdoor vegetable garden surrounded by wildflowers, butterflies, and hummingbirds. Despite working full-time and above minimum wage, money was tight. So when the first fall harvest season came, I accepted an offer and an opportunity to make some money on the side trimming weed. As someone who has always had a deep appreciation for plants and their presence in my life, I found that being surrounded by the actual marijuana plants put me at ease simply by existing for long periods among them.

With time, I gained enough funds, experience, and clout to eventually sponsor my own transformation as a legally compliant grower. I dove into growing medical cannabis as a full-time career. The experience was much like being a scientist, farmer, nurturer, and outlaw, all wrapped into one. My inner circle and community was mostly comprised of female-identifying growers. At that time, women in the cannabis industry were seen as accessories; the stereotype was that women dated the men who grew. We, however, were more than that. And to say I got my hands dirty is an understatement. I hauled around actual tons of dirt and fertilizer, brewed my own buckets of tea with vats of bat and fish guano for my plants. I learned the organic techniques of caring for the cannabis plant, the intricate ways to battle pests, and tricks to organically achieve larger yields. We women traded tips, an essential building block that soon made us experts. With our very own hands, we were growing cannabis for countless patients through co-opted licensed medical distributors. This network of powerful women raised me. These women are still the most influential and important people in my life. Growing cannabis in those years taught me trust, loyalty, science, mathematics, entrepreneurship, confidentiality, and humility.

In spite of my success, the risks of growing weed were still significant even under the California cannabis laws that were made to protect medical consumers and the growers providing their medicine. The difficulties for a cultivator, especially as a person of color, turned me into a recluse. I kept a low and humble profile, but even so, I was often evicted illegally from my home with very little notice.

My fears came to a head one day when my next-door neighbor threatened to call the police about what he described as "suspicious activity" in my home. I was floored. "Are you growing weed?" he asked. My growing operation was legal; I had the certificates hung up on the walls, like the diplomas in a psychologist's office, to prove it. It was strange to me that my neighbor would accuse me like this; the same neighbor whom I would chat with about life and help with yardwork, cleaning up weeds as a gesture of kindness to him and the sick, elderly wife he cared for. The day he confronted me was the day everything changed. Within 30 days, my entire operation was torn down—everything I had worked so hard for was gone, including my home.

My foundation as a cultivator existed in a time when growers and cannabis entrepreneurs weren't able to freely talk about their professions. We were all careful, as very real consequences hovered around us. Now I work with weed in the open, and my clients are comprised of cannabis firms with women in leadership roles. Being transparent about my work within this community has been cathartic, and there's no greater joy.

Weed and Food

When it comes to my advocacy and career within weed, inclusivity is the central theme. Less than 3 percent of people in leadership roles in the cannabis industry look like me—female and black. It's crucial for me to ensure that everyday people like my great auntie Mildred and other older black women can be provided with safe and inexpensive options like cannabis to help them heal during menopause and breast cancer, to find relief from arthritis, or even just for a needed moment of relaxation. That's the driving force behind what I do. *The Art of Weed Butter* as a cookbook brings all of these elements together. It is for those who want and need access to making weed butter to better themselves, the quality of their lives, and the lives of their loved ones.

This cookbook is a cosmic hybrid of my favorite things: cuisine, cannabis, and words. Food is a powerful vehicle and tool for bringing these elements together. Think about the first time you ate something that dramatically changed your perception of that type of cuisine, or culture. Food allows us to be more open-minded about cultures and cannabis. For simple home cooks and world-renowned chefs alike, our fondest experiences in our lives can be traced back to food. In the book *The Cooking Gene: A Journey through African American Culinary History in the Old South*, the dazzling food historian, chef, and author Michael W. Twitty reminds us, "Many of our most pungent memories are carried through food, just as connections to our ancestors are reaffirmed by cooking the dishes handed down to us." The beauty is that food takes no political sides. It's fair, blameless, and is one of the driving forces connecting us to our ancestry.

These sentiments are especially relevant to me as a woman living in Mexico with deep connections to my West African heritage. It's a wild combination through gastronomy. Living here (and eating here) has opened my eyes to the many connections Mexico has to Africa.

In this book are other cultural mash-ups like my mother's signature fried chicken, beans, and white rice, and Mexico's street-food staple, *esquites*—all laced with a low dose of weed (see page 32 for a description of a low dose). Consider this book a celebration of all the ways we are linked and liberated through food. And what better way than with edibles.

INTRODUCTION: WHY COOK WITH WEED BUTTER?

Cannabis sativa, reefer, reggie, weed, pot, herb, trees, ganja, green, loud, marijuana, or medicine. However you refer to it, weed combined with butter is much like liquid gold. For centuries, people have consumed cannabis-infused foods to assist with ailments like pain, lack of appetite, or simply to chill out. The potency of the weed butter you make is up to you. It can be powerful enough to ease chronic pain yet mild enough to allow a gentle mellowness to spread throughout the body and mind—sometimes needed after a stressful day. This versatility is what makes weed butter so great and why I'm here to help you along the way.

Ingesting cannabis as food turns out to be better for your health, especially for those concerned with the effects of smoking. Although the jury is still out on whether resin and smoke from cannabis is responsible for chronic illness, weed butters and oils are the perfect alternative for anyone prudent who prefers to avoid the health side effects (and occasional social stigmas) of smoking weed.

Whether you're adding cannabis-infused butter (also known as cannabutter) into cookies, toast, or boxed macaroni and cheese, it's a multi-use miracle. Inconspicuous and versatile, weed butter is one of the simplest ways to make an edible, and one of the least expensive ways to administer medical marijuana to a patient. Many store-bought edibles contain obscene amounts of sugars and unwanted chemicals. But when making your own cannabutter out of butter or coconut or avocado oil, it can help you recover from the symptoms of chemotherapy or anorexia without unnecessary ingredients that are not suitable for certain patients. And still others can choose to add a recreational drizzle of weed olive oil onto avocado toast for a relaxing Saturday morning. The ways to implement weed butter or oils into your meals are as infinite as the foods we eat.

Eating cannabis-infused butters is a liberating and stigma-free way to consume cannabis; a vehicle to help elevate your mood, relieve pain, or both. Are you on your menstrual cycle and just want a spoonful of weed-infused Nutella to soothe your cramps or satisfy your sweet tooth? Did you have a bad week with work and are hoping to start the weekend with hash browns, bacon, and eggs with a bit of weed? Are you looking for something to alleviate the soreness from yesterday's leg day at the gym? (I'm saying this as if I know what a day at the gym is like, I don't). But either way, we got you—weed butter and I.

Let's take a step back for a moment to think about the power of food. This is a relationship that begins in infancy. Food nourishes us, helps us grow, and has the ability to bring people together in a way that nothing else can. Food is not political; it's not formed by religion or cultural bias. I know what some of you are saying, yes, it can be political, and yes, it has ties to religion and culture, but it didn't start that way, and it is far more universal than that. We are nourished by food, healed by food. It's as simple as that.

What we eat can be seen as the strongest link to our culture. It connects us to where we came from and to where we travel. Growing up in a West African immigrant household, I saw firsthand how the tradition of my parents' country stayed rooted in our everyday lives. So much so that when I finally arrived in Africa, I suffered from very little culture shock and instead made connections that came from a much more innate foundation— mostly informed by the food I ate.

When I speak about food, I'm also referring to all of the herbs, plants, and flowers we eat. I was shocked to learn that broccoli, artichoke, and even plantains are flowers. This tradition of cooking with herbs and flowers has existed since ancient times. It's easy to take for granted the abundance of exotic and nonnative produce, spices, and herbs that

our modern pantries, refrigerators, and spice racks hold. There was a moment in time when all of these things were seen as sacred. That's how I view cooking with cannabis flowers, a.k.a. weed.

Food infused with cannabis has a long association with healing both the body and mind. The types of food we take in, especially superfoods, can help fill the void of what our body is lacking and craving in order to thrive. Nutritionally dense foods, or superfoods (cleverly named by marketers) like broccoli, blueberries, and leafy greens are absorbed to fortify our body with vitamins and nutrients. Cannabis, and by extension tetrahydrocannabinol (THC), could also be considered a superfood.

THC is what most people think of when they think of weed. It gives you the euphoric "high" effects, and can also affect the way you feel pain, hunger, and moods. It can help with inflammation, nausea, and nerve pain, and help increase appetites. No wonder it's used as a treatment for all types of diseases.

Cannabis as an entire plant is the multipurpose food of all foods. We can juice its leaves or grind the seeds to put in smoothies and baked goods. We can use its stalks to make rope, bricks, fuel, cloth, and paper. We dry its flowers to smoke, vape, or create oils to eat or apply directly onto our skin. I know it's corny, but for me, it doesn't get more super than that.

For the past several years as a creative in the cannabis industry, I've worked for the award-winning edibles company, Om Edibles, founded by Maya Elisabeth. Om Edibles has single-handedly pioneered a wide spectrum of uses for cannabis. Many were in disbelief that you could use cannabis oil to help treat lupus, eczema, or even fine lines and wrinkles. Om Edibles has been treating cannabis as a superfood for 10 years, and it goes to show that cannabis is not a passing phase but a medicine that has always been and is here to stay. Whether the leaves are consumed in a green cold press or the oil is drizzled over a salad (I'll show you how to make cannabis-infused balsamic vinaigrette on page 68), taking in a dose of the superfood that is cannabis could be an amazing component of your anti-inflammatory, relaxation, and rejuvenating needs.

When we tap into all the health benefits of cannabis, we unlock and activate receptors in our body's endocannabinoid system. According to modern science, this means that every human body—and some of our four-legged friends, too—are born with receptors that accept more than 100 cannabinoids, like THC and CBD. The Department of Neuroscience at the University of the Basque Country says, "Cannabinoid receptors, located throughout the body, are part of the endocannabinoid system, which is involved in a variety of physiological processes including appetite, pain-sensation, mood, and memory."[1]

When weed is cooked with fat, such as butter, oil, or even bacon grease, you're left with an ingredient that can be effortlessly used as the base for any snack or meal. Perhaps this is to entice your appetite, battle the pain of a cancer patient, or help someone who struggles with PTSD looking for a natural remedy to help them sleep without night terrors.

Combining fat and weed is essentially all you'll need to get started. But you can't just sprinkle your stash onto a recipe like salt; there's more to it than that. Creating truly great weed butter is an art in and of itself. In this book, you will learn the basics of how to extract weed into your coconut oil, fancy French butter from that expensive market, or virtually any fat you prefer. This is a cookbook for grandmothers, stoner bros, stay-at-home parents, soul food enthusiasts, and gourmet chefs alike. Make a small batch of butter for yourself or enough to throw an entire cannabis-infused dinner party. Either way you look at it, it's a dope skill to have (pun intended).

What Is Weed Butter?

Also known as cannabutter, weed butter is one of the most essential components to making edibles. Typically, edibles are made from cannabis-infused fat, sugar, alcohol, or vegetable glycerin. (If you want to learn how to infuse sugar and alcohol, tell my publishers to offer me another book deal!) The fat in butter and oils, however, is the optimal way to transfer the THC from cannabis into an infusion. Turns out, depending on the method you use, you can transfer more than just the THC to the fat, but rather a full spectrum of the chemical components of cannabis. This includes the non-psychoactive properties of THCA, which quietly benefit our health. THCA is similar to CBD, the stuff that doesn't get you high. To learn more about CBD, check out *Healing with CBD: How Cannabidiol Can Transform Your Health without the High*, by Eileen Konieczny.

Let's get back to fat. You know it, the three-letter word that makes most people cringe, that gives us shame and allows us to think we can fat-shame others. It's a substance whose name we've somehow defamed over the years. But it's just not the culprit to bad health and heart disease that we think it is. Fat in itself is not as terrible as we may think.

---

1   Oier Aizpurua-Olaizola, Izaskun Elezgarai, Irantzu Rico-Barrio, Iratxe Zarandona, Nestor Etxebarria, and Aresatz Usobiaga (2016), "Targeting the Endocannabinoid System: Future Therapeutic Strategies." *Drug Discovery Today*, August 20, 2016, https://www.sciencedirect.com/science/article/pii/S1359644616302926.

Here's the thing about fat—it's not actually that bad for you. We need fats, and it's impossible to truly have a healthy diet without them. They keep our skin supple and our hearts functioning better. Think of avocados, fatty oils from fish, and coconut oil. Fat is not only a healthy part of the human diet, but is scientifically the most efficient and most versatile way to infuse weed. Elise McDonough, author of *The Official High Times Cannabis Cookbook,* tells us that "because cannabinoids and fats are both hydrophobic, THC molecules dissolve readily in lipids when they're heated together in a solution. And this friendly relationship continues in your body." There, the psychoactive molecules found in THC take up residence in the fat (adipose) tissues of our bodies and stay in our system for about 30 days. When humans consume THC, it stores itself in the fat cells of our body. So when thinking of how to infuse and extract THC, or even CBD for that matter, it seems perfect to use fat. And which fat is most common in a household? Butter! Which are the optimal fats for your infusion process? Word around the street from most weed cooks is that coconut oil, butter, and bacon grease are the top three best binders (see Chapter Four for recommended oils and fats), followed by olive and avocado oil. But not all fats are the same. Man-made and genetically modified fats like polyunsaturated fatty acids, monounsaturated fats, and trans fats—found in potato chips and fast food—are the culprits behind many health issues. This is mainly because they are foreign to our bodies. And though they can be found in nature, they are usually in very minute traces, which cause little harm. All in all, it's a good idea to use a natural fat, butter, or oil when infusing weed.

Like the brilliant Becky Selengut said in her book, *How to Taste,* "We're literally hardwired to seek out fat and it's foolish to fight it." Fat is one of the best ways to carry THC molecules and full flavor profiles through its spectacular dissolving abilities. Our taste buds, according to Selengut, are unable to truly taste the entire flavor profile of a dish if it lacks the fat from an oil or butter (even the naturally found fats in vegetables and legumes are important for carrying flavor). And when it comes to heat, another essential element in infusing cannabis into a substance, fat is king as a heat transmitter. This will help along the infusion process, making the weed butter infuse evenly. The fat found in butter and oil will regulate the rates at which the infusion occurs, giving you a consistent distribution of potency within the weed butter.

It should also be said that not all infusion processes are the same. Different methods result in different quantities of oil or butter due to the ingredients used. Because butter cooks down more than say, coconut oil, you will be left with a bit less material. Though weed and a fatty substance is all you essentially need, some infusion methods also require a slow cooker, a stovetop, or a binder (the element used to help the weed stick to the substance) such as grain alcohol or protein. Don't get stressed, though, I will take you through each method, step by step. It's not only easier than you think, but having these skills in the kitchen are invaluable and can also be used for just about any herb you might want to infuse. Think rosemary and cannabis-infused butter. From there, you can choose which method, which fat, and which type of weed works best for your lifestyle, given the materials and ingredients you already have on hand.

After infusing, you will be left with weed butter, allowing you to easily incorporate weed to any recipe that requires a little bit of fat. Are you one of those millennial coffee freaks who likes to add a pad of butter to your coffee in the morning? Try it with weed butter. Coffee and a small dose of cannabis (especially CBD) is becoming a popular health tool for sustaining focus throughout the day. Do you like coconut oil in your beans and rice, eggs, or soups? Try some with infused weed. Once you realize how easy it is to make weed butter, you can add it into any meal of your choice—and you'll never want to eat anything without it. However, I don't recommend doing this recreationally. Medically, sure!

The best part about making your own weed butter and edibles is that the potency is up to your personal choice and preference. One pot brownie doesn't have to send you to outer space (unless you're in that kind of mood). Meals prepared with love with the weed butter you'll make from this book can be just enough to help with anxiety or an evening of nightmares from PTSD. The edibles game has completely changed. It's more diverse and healthier than ever before. So much so that *Forbes* confirmed that edibles are not just one of the most enjoyed ways of consuming weed, but that "in California alone, consumers gobbled up more than $180 million worth of marijuana-infused food and drinks in 2016."[2] If you start an edibles business after this, I get it. Go for it, but know that I will ask for a percentage of your profits (I'm kidding).

I am a huge fan of low-dose edibles and microdosing cannabis. A microdose is an approach to studying the behavior of a substance in our bodies through a "subtherapeutic dose of a drug administered at a quantity low enough to elicit no adverse side effects yet high enough for a measurable cellular response."[3] This means a small dose that won't make you feel high but will give you the health benefits needed on a cellular level to help you heal.

---

2   Mike Montgomery, "Edibles Are the Next Big Thing for Pot Entreprenuers." *Forbes Magazine*, July 19, 2017, https://www.forbes.com/sites/mikemontgomery/2017/07/19/edibles-are-the-next-big-thing-for-pot-entrepreneurs/#fd0f6e6576bd.

3   Ayelet Waldman, *A Really Good Day: How Microdosing Made a Mega Difference in My Mood, My Marriage, and My Life*, (New York, NY: Knopf, 2017), 1.

A small dose is unlikely to produce whole-body psychoactive effects. Less is more: more fun and less intense. It allows you to actually eat and enjoy the edibles you make, because you know what? Food is pretty damn enjoyable. The low-dose recipe options allow you to savor the food's taste while enjoying the benefits of weed-infused foods without feeling crazy high. In the book, we will talk about how to decide which dose, which strain of weed, and which type of fat to choose for all of your cannabis-infused cooking needs. And as you know, weed butter is not limited to just butter but I love butter so allow me to just keep rolling with that—another pun intended. That's the last one, I promise.

How to Use this Book

The majority of us infusing weed butter and cooking with cannabis are stoners—highly functioning and highly successful stoners, but stoners nonetheless. No shame! I'm not entirely sure when or how the stoner, slacker stereotype became associated with people who consume cannabis. In fact, studies show that despite the "stereotypical stoner humor, cannabis consumers have been shown to be more intelligent than their non-consuming counterparts. And that applies especially to women. According to a new study, women who smoke weed have higher IQs than those who don't."[4] But for humor and the sake of better organization, let's just say that we are all stoners who are forgetful and need extra help when it comes to directions. And what's better for a stoner than a quick reference guide? This section is your holy grail if you need a reminder of where things are located in the book.

This cookbook is intended to be your go-to guide for everything cannabutter related. Whether you're grabbing your favorite box of store-bought brownie mix or taking it up a notch with my mom's fried chicken recipe (see page 74), all the info you'll need will be here to help you whip up truly elevated food. I've organized the book into a couple of different chapters so you can easily refer back to them whenever you need.

---

4   Madison Margolin, "Women with Higher IQs Are More Likely to Smoke Weed." *Jane Street*, October 3, 2017, https://janest.com/article/2017/10/03/women-higher-iqs-likely-smoke-weed.

Chapter One starts with a microdose (see what I did there?) overview of the history of edibles, marijuana, and a couple of lightweight trailblazers who laid the groundwork for cannabis cuisine in modern mainstream culture. I cover the medical, legal, and cultural components of what it means to ingest, inhale, and take pride in cooking with weed.

Cannabis is medicine, and sometimes it's prudent to treat it as such. I dedicated Chapter Two to walking you through how to dose weed butter and associate each milligram of dosage with a level of "high." There are days you only want to eat a 2-milligram THC spoonful of weed-infused Nutella, but sometimes you need more. There will be days where you just want to sit on a sofa and eat enough edibles to rid you of a terrible bout of cramps. You'll figure out which dosage and what recipes work for treating minor ailments, managing mood, or managing your pain. The important thing to understand is that it's your choice and your body, and you have full freedom.

You'll also learn how eating weed affects your body, and sometimes your mind, differently than smoking weed does. If you're a connoisseur or just a very detail-oriented Virgo and want to nerd out with pairing strains for weed-infused butter or coconut oil, there's a section for this on page 28. Find a basic chart guiding you through which flavor profiles and terpenes you might expect from a strain of weed and which dish each terpene teams up with deliciously. Don't know what terpenes are? Don't care about pairing? Not a big deal. I've tried all types of strains with different butters, oils, and fats, and trust me, they all taste incredible.

In Chapter Three, we get right to a very comprehensive step-by-step guide to multiple infusion methods and different types of weed butter. Whatever equipment you have on hand, there is an infusion method that will work for you. And before I get on with the actual recipes, in Chapter Four, you will learn to identify which type of oil, butter, or fat to use in your infusion batch.

Now, let's get started!

Chapter *One*

WEED 101

The First Edible

Humans have a long history with consuming cannabis. Emperor Shen Nung from 2737 BCE, also known as the father of Chinese medicine, was known to use cannabis as a medicine. He was also known to be an excellent steward of the land and showed compassion and concern for his people who suffered from illness. "According to legend, he compiled the medical encyclopedia called *Pen Ts'ao*. The *Pen Ts'ao* lists hundreds of drugs derived from vegetable, animal, and mineral sources. Among these drugs is the plant cannabis, [named] "ma."[5]

The history of edibles—food containing weed—dates back as early as 1000 BC. Before the "space cake" or "pot brownie," in the region of South Asia there was bhang. Bhang is a preparation of cannabis in a form both ingested as a food and drink. Like a thick ganja smoothie, it was known to have been originally made in the ancient subcontinent of India, used during the spring festival of Holi both for medicinal and spiritual purposes. And what better occasion than the entering of spring to celebrate with an edible? The birds are chirping, the earth is blooming and rebirthing herself, and so is your consciousness and potential for healing.

Bhang is packed with an all-star lineup of nutritiously fortifying ingredients similar to what you might find in chai: milk, masala, cinnamon, anise, rose water, honey, sugar, and weed. This energy cannabis drink was recommended for various health reasons. It was given to ancient Indian newlyweds who were looking to increase their libido, to ancient warriors trying to calm their nerves before a brutal battle, and to patients battling the life-threatening symptoms of malaria. With a wide range of beneficial and healing properties, despite current federal and international regulations toward marijuana, it's no wonder that we are still to this day consuming food infused with cannabis for its health reasons.

The First Pot Brownie

The first time cannabis appeared in a cookbook was in 1954, when the epic Alice B. Toklas published her "Hashish Fudge" pot brownie in *The Alice B. Toklas Cookbook*. Her pot brownie recipe was borrowed from the brilliant and successful painter, writer, sound poet, and performance artist, Brion Gysin. It has a glorious funky mix of spices, nuts, fruit, and our bestie, weed. My pot brownie recipe on page 91 is a nod to this original

---

5   Jann Gumbiner Ph.D, "History of Cannabis in Ancient China." *Psychology Today*, May 10, 2011, https://www.psychologytoday.com/us/blog/the-teenage-mind/201105/history-cannabis-in-ancient-china.

version. Either make the brownie mix from scratch and re-create your favorite recipe, or add it to your favorite store-bought boxed mix. I don't judge, but I do recommend you add a handful of buttery cashews whether it's a box or from scratch. Unless you're allergic to nuts—then please don't do that.

Alice, a San Francisco native with Polish Jewish heritage, shared an abundant life as a writer and a beautiful partnership with girlfriend, Gertrude Stein, in France. There, they were known to throw salons and cooked for some of their besties, including Ernest Hemingway, Matisse, and Picasso—yes, I said Picasso. If this isn't the ultimate inspiration for you to throw a weed dinner party tonight, nothing else in this book will do it.

My other favorite OG in the weed cookbook game was Chef Ra, born as Jim Wilson Jr. in West Virginia. Chef Ra is pretty well-known to the old heads in the cannabis community, but his clout came from his Psychedelic Kitchen column that was featured in the *High Times* magazine for 15 years.

Medical Cannabis

Medical cannabis administered in the form of edibles is by and large considered one of the best alternatives to expensive, overprescribed, and highly addictive pain medications. "Medical marijuana has been shown to be an effective treatment for pain that may also reduce the chance of opioid dependence," said Dr. Howard Zucker, the New York State Health Commissioner. "Adding opioid replacement as a qualifying condition for medical marijuana offers providers another treatment option, which is a critical step in combating the deadly opioid epidemic affecting people across the state."[6]

According to the American Nurses Association, all types of marijuana, including cannabinoids such as THC, CBD, CBN, THCA, and others, have been widely used medically to treat certain diseases and/or suppress symptoms. "It has been used for alleviating symptoms of nausea and vomiting; stimulating appetite in HIV patients; alleviating chronic pain; easing spasticity due to multiple sclerosis; decreasing symptoms of depression, anxiety, sleep disorders and psychosis; and relieving intraocular pressure from glaucoma."[7] This

---

6   New York State Department of Health, "New York State Department of Health Announces Opioid Replacement Now a Qualifying Condition for Medical Marijuana," The Official Website of New York State, July 2018, https://www.health.ny.gov/press/releases/2018/2018-07-12_opioid_replacement.htm.

7   ANA Center for Ethics and Human Rights, "Therapeutic Use of Marijuana and Related Cannabinoids," American Nurses Association, 2016, https://www.nursingworld.org/~49a8c8/globalassets/practiceandpolicy/ethics/therapeutic-use-of-marijuana-and-related-cannabinoids-position-statement.pdf.

means that something as simple and delicious as a weed pancake or salad with infused olive oil can provide just as much or more pain relief as an expensive prescribed drug.

As the positive benefits of cannabis begin to swell into common, mainstream knowledge, and as we learn that these benefits outweigh the risks (are there any risks other than extreme munchies and sleepiness?), we see more headway in academic studies. Many labs are increasing their research in this area. In June 2018, the United Nations Drug Committee had its first ever meeting to address, analyze, and discuss the safety and health benefits of cannabis. Here's what they found: Cannabis is a "relatively safe drug"[8] that millions of people have already been using globally to help manage a wide range of medical conditions.[9] I know what you're thinking: "Duh."

Cannabis and Modern Times

Sixty-one percent of the US bipartisan population supports the legalization of recreational marijuana, with even more people in solidarity supporting medicinal marijuana. Unfortunately, the reefer madness propaganda from the early twentieth century still plagues the nation. Despite legalization in many states, many people are still arrested for the possession of weed. Modern history shows that we have a fickle and unforgiving legal relationship with marijuana.

In the early 1900s, cannabis was widely prescribed in the United States until about 1937, when the Marihuana Tax Act was introduced. One of the strongest supporters of this prohibition and the criminalization of drugs was Harry Anslinger, the United States Commissioner and Treasurer of the Federal Bureau of Narcotics. He stated among his colleagues that "reefer makes darkies think they're as good as white men." This was the tone that played a pivotal role in cannabis prohibition.

These beliefs crystalized for decades. In 1970, the Controlled Substances Act was passed, declaring marijuana as a Schedule 1 drug. This means that at this moment, according to federal law, cannabis is described as a drug "with a high potential for abuse, a drug with

---

8   Expert Committee on Drug Dependence, "Cannabidiol Critical Review Report," World Health Organization, June 7, 2018, http://www.who.int/medicines/access/controlled-substances/WHOCBDReportMay2018-2 .pdf?ua=1.
9   Sara Brittany Somerset, "UN Drug Committee Finds Cannabis an Effective, 'Relatively Safe Drug,'" Leafly, June 11, 2018, https://www.leafly.com/news/politics/un-drug-committee-finds-cannabis-an-effective-relatively-safe-drug.

no currently accepted medical use in treatment in the United States, and a drug for which there is a lack of accepted safety for use under medical supervision."[10]

In the United States, drugs, substances, and certain chemicals used to make drugs are classified into five distinct categories or schedules depending upon the drug's acceptable medical use and its potential for abuse or dependence. The abuse rate is a determining factor in the scheduling of the drug; for example, Schedule 1 drugs (including heroin, LSD, and cocaine) are said to have a high potential for abuse and the potential to create severe psychological and/or physical dependence. According to the law, as the drug schedule decreases—Schedule 2, Schedule 3, etc.—so does the abuse potential.[11] Marijuana is still a Schedule 1 drug, despite it being legal and used medically in most states.[12]

The Controlled Substances Act was a vehicle to unofficially villainize mostly Mexican immigrants and people of color while shaping the war on drugs. John Hudak of the *Washington Post* wrote that "marijuana's strict scheduling emerges from the cultural and racial apathy felt by Richard Nixon who signed the Controlled Substances Act into law. Nixon's aides suggested the war on marijuana was racially motivated, and Oval Office tapes highlight his contempt for the counterculture movement as well as racial minorities."[13]

On December 1, 1975, when the Supreme Court ruled it was "not cruel or unusual for Ohio to sentence someone to 20 years for having or selling cannabis,"[14] the message was heard loud and clear.

In January 2018, days after California officially legalized cannabis with Proposition 64, Attorney General Jeff Sessions made an official and disarming announcement stating that he would be encouraging the Justice Department to increase law enforcement for marijuana, particularly in jurisdictions that have legalized cannabis.

---

10   Legal Information Institute, "21 U.S. Code § 812 - Schedules of Controlled Substances," Cornell Law School, https://www.law.cornell.edu/uscode/text/21/812.

11   United States Department of Justice. "DEA Drug Scheduling," https://www.dea.gov/druginfo/ds.shtml.

12   American RSDHope, "Schedules or Classes of Drugs," www.rsdhope.org/schedule-or-classes-of-drugs .html.

13   John Hudak, "How Racism and Bias Criminalized Marijuana," *Washington Post*, April 28, 2016, https://www.washingtonpost.com/news/in-theory/wp/2016/04/28/how-racism-and-bias-criminalized-marijuana/?utm_term=.1169a62032be.

14   NBC News Archive, "Supreme Court/Marijuana/Busing/Abortion" Vanderbilt Television News Archive, originally aired December 1, 1975, retrieved March 9, 2011, https://tvnews.vanderbilt.edu/broadcasts/35203.

More than one person is arrested every minute for marijuana possession in this country. An astounding 574,641 people were arrested for simple marijuana possession in the United States in 2016—that's 89 percent of all marijuana-related arrests. Remember that these aren't dealers, distributors, or kingpins. They are just everyday people with a little bit of weed.[15]

In 2016, the *Washington Post* reported that more people were arrested for weed than for murder, rape, aggravated assault, and robbery *combined*. According to the ACLU, people of color were anywhere from four to eight times more likely to be arrested for marijuana than their white peers, despite the fact that statistically, white folks consume cannabis at slightly higher rates than people of color do.[16]

If this sounds both confusing and ridiculous to you, you're not alone. In California, Colorado, Alaska, Nevada, Washington, Oregon, Massachusetts, Maine, and Washington, D.C., marijuana is legalized for both recreational and medical use. Meanwhile, there are currently 30 states in the United States that have passed medical marijuana bills of some sort. However, even with these laws in place, many are arrested for cannabis.

Sorry for the Buzzkill

I do apologize if sharing these crucial facts have killed your vibe—or your high. One buys a weed butter cookbook to cook weed butter, not feel preached at. But cooking with cannabis and enjoying cannabis is so much bigger than that. It's a right that we have as people to heal ourselves in the way we choose without hurting ourselves, without hurting other people, and without the prejudice and injustices that sometimes occur from consuming cannabis alone.

My intentions come from a place of advocacy. Without advocacy and sharing the facts, we would not be where we are today. In knowing, we are able to better enjoy and understand our privilege while using it to fight for those who cannot. Being a well-informed consumer is an integral tool to help us understand how we've evolved, what has worked in the past, and what isn't working now. It informs our decisions when we vote and how we address these topics at home and in our communities.

---

15   Shaun King, "Despite Liberalizing Marijuana Laws, the War on Drugs Still Targets People of Color." The Intercept, January 25, 2018, https://theintercept.com/2018/01/25/marijuana-legalization-weed-drug-arrest.
16   ACLU. "Marijuana Arrests by the Numbers," https://www.aclu.org/gallery/marijuana-arrests-numbers.

Chapter *Two*

EDIBLE HEALTH

You're probably reading this book because you're interested in edibles as a healthy alternative to the intense and potential long-term consequences of smoking weed. As we've covered, edibles are a go-to for people looking for lasting relief to their chronic pain and other severe medical symptoms.

If health is really your concern, the fried chicken or cobbler recipes, though delicious, don't have to be all that you make. Try adding some infused olive oil into a salad, or add a dose of weed to any super healthy and delicious dish that calls for coconut oil. Though I tried to curate a nice balance of healthy and easy recipes in this cookbook, know that there are plenty of possibilities for making healthy infused-cannabis dishes. You can get creative.

Eating Weed Butter vs. Smoking Weed

The liver runs through it. Ever wonder why, when eating edibles or weed butter, it takes longer to feel the high? It's because the weed takes a couple extra steps before entering our bloodstream. First it goes to the stomach, then our liver. The process can take up to three hours before our bodies feel the full effect. Bailey Rahn, an editor at Leafly, reminds us that "THC is metabolized by the liver, which converts it to 11-hydroxy-THC. This active metabolite is particularly effective in crossing the blood-brain barrier, resulting in a more intense high."[17] Smoking, however, goes through the lungs and immediately into the bloodstream, giving us that quicker, instantly gratifying high that we're more accustomed to.

Be patient. I can't stress this enough, but as a very important rule of thumb, when consuming edibles, start slow. Some may feel the effects of the cannabis within 30 minutes, others not until three hours later. When testing your weed butter, test about ¼ teaspoon of the weed butter you make, or approximately one serving of your cannabis-

---

17 Bailey Rahn, "Ingest or Inhale? 5 Differences Between Cannabis Edibles and Flowers." Leafly, July 17, 2014, https://www.leafly.com/news/cannabis-101/differences-between-marijuana-edibles-and-flower.

infused dish. Wait about an hour. Take note of how you feel and let your body tell you whether this is a good amount, if you need more, or if you need less. Erring on the side of caution will ensure that you actually enjoy yourself and have a positive experience.

Experiment to find the perfect dose. This book will help you achieve an almost perfect dose, but know that edibles rarely have exactly the same potency from piece to piece, even when store bought. Not every single batch of butter or oil will be the same, unless they are tested by a laboratory. It will be difficult for you to ensure that each batch will be exactly the same. Perhaps the last batch was really mild and you want to double the serving into a dish that you are cooking or baking. While I encourage you to experiment with what potency works best for you, test each batch of butter ahead of time before baking to ensure the most accuracy possible for the dish.

Did You Get Too High?

Too stoned and don't know what to do? Because I care deeply about you and don't want you to get turned off to edibles, here are a couple of tips and tricks I've learned throughout the years to mellow out your buzz. These tips also work for folks who've smoked too much. The most important thing to remember is that we've all been there, and this too shall pass.

1. Eat citrus and/or pepper. The beta-myrcene terpene in black pepper helps you feel at ease. Also, the acid and limonene terpenes (we'll get more into terpenes on page 28) found in limes, oranges, and grapefruits can help reduce the effects of THC. Be sure you eat that pulp and try getting a little lemon zest in—it's the most important part. If you have the gumption, try recreating an elixir I copped from Simone Fischer[18] to help ease the feeling of being too stoned. The mint and ginger will help your stomach calm down while giving you some pep.

Citrus Mint Pepper Fizzle

To a glass of sparkling water or club soda, add ¼ teaspoon freshly ground black peppercorns, the juice and zest of one lemon or lime, a few springs of fresh mint, and optionally, some freshly grated ginger. Add ice and serve immediately.

---

18 Simone Fischer, "Too Stoned? How to Manage Being Uncomfortably High." Ladybud, February 8, 2016, http://www.ladybud.com/2016/02/08/too-stoned-how-to-manage-being-uncomfortably-high.

2. Avoid sweets or fats. As you read earlier, THC is transferred and stored in fats. It's also stored in sugars, although the rate isn't as high as with fats. Try a savory snack instead, perhaps one that you can squeeze a lime on.

3. Hydration station. Carbonated water works wonders. I don't know if this is scientific, but somehow, the bubbles during those super-high moments help me calm down. Drinking plenty of water is always a good idea for overall health and doubles as an agent to battle cottonmouth (dry mouth).

4. Take a nap. Don't judge, but I once ate an edible that three hours later made me feel way too high. I was set to meet up with a friend for a work-related event in just one hour. So what did I do? I decided to take a quick nap. I woke up 20 minutes later and felt brand new, as if I hadn't eaten an edible at all. Any sort of relaxation is key, but a 30- to 45-minute nap is ideal and will make you feel refreshed.

5. Cold showers. Known to lower other things *cough*, a cold shower can take your attention away from the high while also closing your pores (yes, I care about my pores). But avoid a hot shower or bath, as the steam will heighten the feelings of euphoria and lightheadedness.

6. Chill out. Relax. Just remember that you're going to be fine. You're not going to die and nothing terrible is going to happen to you. If anything, once it's all said and done, the unnoticed benefits of cannabis have no doubt helped you and your body in ways undetectable to you.

Weed Pairings and Terpenes

As we continue to discover more about cannabis, we've learned that different strains of cannabis have unique characteristics, similar to those of wine. Some strains make you feel more relaxed while others help you focus. Terpenes are one of the signifiers for those characteristics. How does it taste and smell? Is your weed sweet or is it fruity? Does it have strong hints of citrus or is it more piney? What you smell from these flowery buds are the terpene profiles.

Terpenes, Effects, and Flavor Profiles

Terpene	Strains	Taste profile	Effects	Helps/Used as	Dish pairing
Linalool	Purple Kush, Lavender, Sour Kush	Floral	Relaxing	Insomnia, stress, depression, anxiety, pain	Green Ganja Dressing (page 69), Classic Weed Balsamic Vinaigrette (page 68)
Myrcene	Mango Kush, Trainwreck, Grape Ape, Granddaddy Purple	Mixed herbal and citrus, musk	Relaxing, psychoactive, calming	Antiseptic, antibacterial, antifungal, inflammation	Elevated Avocado Toast (page 62), Mennlay's Medicated Fried Plantains (page 88)
Limonene	OG Kush, Jack Herer, Lemon Haze	Orange, lemon, lime	Mood elevation, stress relief	Depression, anxiety, gastric reflux, antifungal	Baked sweets, Fluffy Medicated Blueberry Mini-Cakes (page 61), Nutty Vegan Chipotle Aioli (page 67), Morning Medicated Fruit Bowl (page 55)
Pinene A and B	Blue Dream, Afghani Kush, Bay Dream	Sweet, sharp, pine, sage	Alertness	Focus, memory attention, inflammation, asthma	Garlic-Crunch Sweet Potato Fries (page 76), Easy Cheese Cannabis Spinach Frittata (page 57), Summer Squash Lasagna (page 79), Cute and Cheesy Macaroni Bake (page 72)
Trans-caryophyllene	Chemdog, Sour Diesel, Bubba Kush, Fire OG	Spicy, peppery, woody	Not known for obvious physical effects	Inflammation, muscle pains and spasms, and insomnia	West African Fried Chicken (page 74), Philly Jalapeño Crema (page 65), Chacahua Coconut Beans and Rice (page 81)

Terpenes are found all over the natural world in countless herbs, plants, trees, and even a select group of insects. They are known to be a key component to various plant resins— cannabis is no exception. Scientifically speaking, "terpenes belong to a class of compounds known as aromatic hydrocarbons that are made up of chains of linked isoprene units. Isoprene is an abundant naturally occurring molecule with the chemical formula C_5H_8, and terpenes are formed by two or more linked isoprene units."[19] The strong aroma of terpenes wards off potential predators and attracts others that may help the plant to

---

19 "What Are Terpenes?" Prohbtd, Accessed September 11, 2018, https://prohbtd.com/index.php/what-are-terpenes.

fight off other pests. For example, in some outdoor cannabis gardens, you may see an abundance of lady bugs and frogs who are attracted to the terpenes. The lady bugs and frogs then eat troublesome bugs that will otherwise destroy the plant and possibly the entire crop.

Though there are around 100 different types of terpenes in the Cannabis sativa species the most common flavor profiles are sweet, spicy, citrus, and herbal. Each terpene is responsible for creating a different effect on your body or mood. It's not necessary to think about terpenes, but they are something you might want to consider when choosing which strain of marijuana you want to use for your weed butter infusions.

Have fun with it. Consider terpene pairing to be an added dimension to the butter and dish you choose to make—an opportunity to get creative with a desired effect or taste. On page 29, I've listed a little guide to terpenes and suggest which recipes might pair well with certain profiles. Not in the mood to nerd out on this? Not a problem, I get it. No matter what strain of cannabis you choose to use, your cannabutter is going to taste incredible. Just remember that regardless of whether you're using cannabis flower, trim, or shake, quality is everything. The more crystals (trichomes), the better. Again, these are only suggestions. But if you're down to experiment, try it out and let me know what works best with which meals. I'd love to hear about your pairing. Leave me a note at my website, www.mennlay.com.

Dosing Cannabutter and Weed Oil

Let's be real: When it comes to edibles, most people make them far stronger than necessary. It's both a waste of precious cannabis, and in my personal opinion, a gluttonous way to treat a sacred plant. It might be a good idea to remember that cannabis has the capacity to be a strong medicine, hence the existence of medical marijuana. But I'm not here to preach, just to inform you that when it comes to making weed butter, less is more.

The horror stories associated with strong edibles are the only reason why edibles get such a bad rap. Everyone has that story—"I ate this edible and got sooooo high that I [blank]." This is unfortunate, considering how many more people could find relief or enjoyment with edibles, if they ate them responsibly.

How does one eat edibles responsibly? Well, by consuming the amount of cannabis that your body can physically and mentally handle. The good news is that you can never technically overdose on weed. And if you do it right, finding your perfect dose can be quite valuable and fun. (If you do get too high, try one of my tips on page 27.) Schedule a day or an evening to test your dosage sweet spot. When testing, consider your energy levels, emotional state, and daily workload. Despite the fact that I've consumed cannabis for 21 years, I'm a lightweight and prefer lower doses at or around 5 to 10 mg. What does that feel like? Here's a handy breakdown:

THC (mg)	Dose	Effects
0–2	Microdose	No noticeable euphoric effect.
3–5	Low	Minimal noticeable euphoric effect.
6–10	Minimum	This is on the lower side of what most legal and medical states consider to be a standard dose. Small euphoric effect.
11–15	Standard	This is your standard dose, 10 mg being the sweet spot. Moderate euphoric effect.
16–25	Experienced	Normal dose for an experienced user. Strong euphoric effect.
26–80	Very experienced	Very high dose, for intense pain relief.
81–100	Expert	Extremely high dose best administered by health professionals.
101+	Medical	Extremely high dose that should only be administered by health professionals.

Potency Chart

More than just a trend, microdosing and low dosing are an integral part of my personal philosophy when smoking, vaping, or eating edibles. I like to keep my THC serving sizes low. What's the point of making tasty edibles if you can't eat every last crumb? Eating in lower doses allows you to enjoy a full meal without feeling uncomfortably high. Each cannabis oil recipe in this book starts with either 7 grams (¼ ounce) or 14 grams (½ ounce) of weed. This loosely translates into about 15 mg or 30 mg of THC, respectively, for each teaspoon of oil or butter used in the entire dish.

When testing for potency, remember that it will take some time for you to feel the effects and benefits of your cannabutter, canna-oil, or cannabis-infused food. When you eat an edible, unlike when you smoke a joint, the cannabis enters your bloodstream through your gut. This means that the THC or CBD gets absorbed at a slower rate than it does when smoking or vaping. Sometimes you might feel a more intense body high. As a rule of thumb, wait one to two hours to see how you feel before eating a second serving of your medicated meal. Try to do this on a day when you're able to chill out, in case you find that you've gotten too stoned.

Below is a handy chart to use when deciding on the potency of your weed butter. In this book, all recipes use the lowest dose, meaning that for every cup of weed butter or weed oil, there will be 700 mg of THC. Remember that 1 cup = 8 ounces = 48 teaspoons. If you've had a serving and don't feel anything after two hours, it's okay to try some more.

Weed Butter Potency

Dose	Quantity of weed, before infusion	%THC/strain	Infused butter, oil, or fat	THC or CBD/cup	THC or CBD (mg)/teaspoon
Low dose	¼ ounce (7g)	10 percent	1 cup/2 sticks	700 mg	14.58
Moderate dose	½ ounce (14g)	10 percent	1 cup/2 sticks	1400 mg	29.17
Potent dose	1 ounce (28g)	10 percent	1 cup/2 sticks	2800 mg	53.33

The average strain of marijuana will contain approximately 10 percent of THC. However, different strains may have different percentages of THC and/or CBD. Take note of the labels on weed purchased from a dispensary or retailer, which should list the percentage. If they do not, find out the name or strain—it's always a good idea to know which strain you are using. If you know the name of your weed, you can easily look it up online. I know, the internet, right? On a secure device, simply search for the strain followed by "percentage of THC." Leafly.com is a great resource for this. If a strain is over 10 percent THC, add 70 extra milligrams for each additional percentage point. For example, if a strain is 11% THC and you infuse 1 cup of butter with 7 grams of cannabis, it will be 770 milligrams of THC total in the entire batch. Similarly, you would wind up with 840 milligrams for a 12% strain, 1050 milligrams for a 15% strain, and so on. If your preferred cannabis strain is CBD dominant, use the same calculations above to reflect amounts of CBD in your infusion.

If you find that after testing, the batch of weed butter or oil you made was too weak for your preference, feel free to increase the grams of weed by increments of 7 to more easily calculate potency. For example, if the standard dose of 14 grams (½ ounce) is too low for you, but you don't want to add an entire ounce, just increase the amount of weed you're using by 7 grams for a total of 21 grams of cannabis—that's ¾ ounce.

If you find that the batch is too strong, dilute your batch by adding one additional cup of butter, oil, or fat to your infusion, and mix evenly by shaking and stirring. Once it is cooled, try one teaspoon of the new mix and see how your body feels.

Storage

You know this one: Store in a cool, dry, and dark place. Pretty standard, right? Be sure to contain your weed butter and cannabis-infused oils and fats in a tightly sealed container or jar. I suggest glass jars with metal or plastic lids. Because your butter, oil, or fat is infused with cannabis, there is a chance that the potency of the infusion might degrade after two to three months, degrading more each time the container is exposed to air, sun, or light. And, as always, please keep your infusions out of the reach of children or pets. Here are some more specific storage tips:

Cannabutter: Well-sealed mason jar or container. Lasts up to six months refrigerated or frozen.

Cannabis Oil: Well-sealed mason jar or container. Lasts up to one year.

Cannabis Fats: Keep in a well-sealed mason jar. Can last from one to three months.

Chapter *Three*

INFUSING CANNABIS

This is the part that you've been waiting for! I hope it was worth all that nerdy foreplay you had to read through in the previous sections.

As it turns out, there are a million ways to extract the healing properties of weed into oil, butter, or fat. But it's important to find a method that works best for you. You don't have to be a master chef or cannabis connoisseur to make great weed butter. You just need to be well-informed, patient, and organized. Most folks who are looking to make edibles are patients or people who want to medicate independently, discreetly, and inexpensively. We're all just everyday folks looking for an efficient way to get high, so don't feel daunted by this at all. In the following pages, I've broken down the most trusted methods based on various desired aspects, such as potency, odor, simplicity, and cost. Have fun, and remember to use a timer, even if you're not stoned.

DECARBOXYLATION

The first thing you'll have to do, regardless of which method you're using, is decarboxylate your cannabis material. Also known as "decarbing," this requires you to bake your weed, allowing the THC or CBD to activate. Raw, unsmoked cannabis contains various cannabinoids, including THCA and CBDA. These cannabinoids need to be heated in order to turn into THC or CBD. This happens when you smoke a joint, for example. It's an instant decarboxylation that helps you to achieve your high. THCA is great for you too, but it won't give you the same effects as THC. Decarbing is a necessary step in order to enjoy the full spectrum of the cannabis you consume. Also, it allows for the lipids (such as fatty acids, waxes, and some vitamins) in the butter or oils to easily bind to your weed for the ultimate cannabis infusion.

Though you can use top-notch, beautiful cannabis flowers from your local dispensary, feel free to use trimmings, stems, and/or stalks. If you're someone who cultivates weed, it's a great way to cut back on waste while using the entire plant. Just be sure that the quality of the plant is clean (free of pesticides, mold, etc.) and that the material is frosty with some trichomes.

WHAT YOU'LL NEED

desired amount of weed (¼ ounce, ½ ounce, or 1 ounce)

hand grinder or scissors

glass baking dish or sheet pan

oven

WHAT TO DO

1. Preheat the oven to 220°F.

2. Gently break apart the desired amount of weed using a hand-grinder, scissors, or with hands until it's the perfect consistency for rolling a joint—fine, but not too fine. Anything too fine will slip through cheesecloth (or a joint, for that matter).

You want your cannabutter and oil to be clean and as clear as possible.

3. Evenly spread your plant material onto the glass baking dish or sheet pan. Pop in the oven on the center rack for 20 minutes if using old or lower quality weed; 45 minutes for cured, high-

grade weed; or 1 hour or more for anything that has been recently harvested and is still wet.

4. Check on the weed frequently while it's in the oven, gently mixing it every 10 minutes so as to not burn it. You will notice that the color of your herb will change from bright green to a deep brownish green. That's when you know it has decarboxylated.

Just so you know, while you're decarbing, your kitchen will smell like one giant edible. I love the way it smells, personally. But if you're worried about neighbors, close windows and burn incense, palo santo, sage, candles, or whatever you prefer. Another great idea is to cook or bake something while your weed is decarbing. The other aromas will fill your home as well.

CLARIFIED BUTTER

Though not absolutely important, clarifying butter beforehand can result in a more even consistency of weed butter. Similar to ghee, clarified butter is butterfat that has been separated from milk solids and water.

WHAT YOU'LL NEED
8–16 ounces butter

saucepan

mason jar or air-tight container

spoon

WHAT TO DO
1. In a medium saucepan, heat your butter over medium-low heat until it melts.

2. Once it's fully melted into a liquid, gently skim the white milk solids and any water from the top of the butter with a spoon. Use in your infused cannabutter recipe, or transfer clarified butter into a mason jar or air-tight container for later use.

INFUSION WITH ALCOHOL

Tamar Wise, a biochemist and CEO of Wise Science Consulting, has called this method of extraction the "scientific method." It includes using your preferred brand of unflavored grain alcohol, such as Everclear. Adding the alcohol is what makes it scientific. Alcohol helps to break down the cellulose, a major construction component of most green plants. With weed, this breakdown allows for the activated THC or CBD to bind better to your butter, oil, or fat. I used avocado oil for this recipe, but you can use any type of fat.

Time: 6½ hours ✻ *Appeal:* High THC extraction ✻ *Yield:* 12 tablespoons

WHAT YOU'LL NEED

1 ounce grain alcohol

½ ounce decarboxylated cannabis material (page 36)

spray bottle or shot glass and spoon

8 ounces clarified butter (page 37), melted butter, oil, or fat

slow cooker

spoon

cheesecloth

storage container of choice

WHAT TO DO

1. Pour 1 ounce of grain alcohol directly onto your decarboxylated marijuana. You can use a spray bottle to evenly distribute the alcohol among the decarbed cannabis, or you can use a 1-ounce shot glass and small spoon, which is what I did.

2. Once the weed is completely saturated with the alcohol, let it sit for 15 to 20 minutes.

3. Add the butter, oil, or fat directly into the slow cooker. Then, add the cannabis into the slow cooker and stir with a spoon until completely incorporated.

4. Put the lid on the slow cooker and let it cook on low for 6 hours. After 6 hours, there will be a glossy, glass-like top coat.

5. Secure a cheesecloth over your preferred storage container and strain the mixture through it.

6. Be sure that the infusion is completely cool before placing it into a refrigerator or freezer.

INFUSION WITH LECITHIN

As it turns out, lecithin protein does wonders during the extraction process of cannabutter or oil. Though optional, a batch made with either sunflower lecithin or soy lecithin is best when cooking something with a sweet profile. Why? Lecithin, sometimes used as a nutritional supplement, is a fat naturally found in many foods like soybeans, eggs, and avocado. This is an emulsifier that helps to bind all of the ingredients together, allowing for potential increase in the potency of your oil or butter. There are a lot of steps in this process, but it's totally worth it if you have the ingredients on hand.

Time: 5½ hours ❋ *Appeal:* Low Potency ❋ *Yield:* 12 tablespoons

WHAT YOU'LL NEED

½ ounce decarboxylated cannabis material (page 36)

½ cup lecithin or soy lecithin

8 ounces clarified butter (page 37), melted butter, oil, or fat

oven

shallow glass baking dish

spatula

wooden spoon or masher

aluminum foil

freezer

cheesecloth

storage container of choice

WHAT TO DO

1. Preheat the oven to 215°F.

2. Evenly spread ½ ounce of ground cannabis flowers in a shallow glass baking dish.

3. Tightly cover the dish with aluminum foil to seal in all the vapors from your weed. Then, place in the oven for about 20 minutes.

4. Take the dish out of the oven, leaving on the foil. Let cool for about 20 more minutes.

5. Lightly and evenly, sprinkle the lecithin onto the cannabis followed by your clarified butter. Mix with a spatula until the consistency is even.

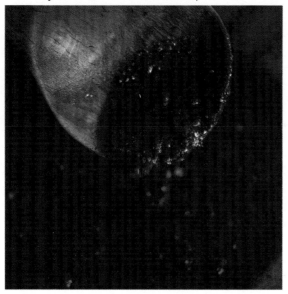

6. Tightly wrap the foil around the dish and put back into the oven for 45 minutes.

7. Remove the dish from the oven and gently take off the foil, being careful not to burn yourself. Gently press the butter or oil mixture with a masher or wooden spoon.

8. Put the foil back on and place the dish back in the oven for 45 minutes.

9. After 45 minutes, remove the dish from the oven, let cool completely, and if needed, transfer into a freezer-safe glass dish. Put the foil onto the new dish and put in the freezer for 2½ hours.

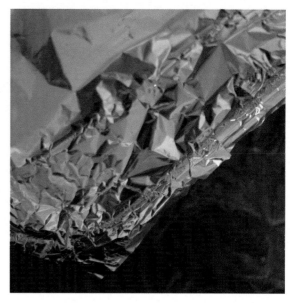

10. Remove your dish and let it defrost to room temperature. Preheat the oven to 215°F.

11. Make sure the dish is completely cool to avoid breaking your dish and ruining all the oil. Once it has thawed to room temperature, place in the oven for just enough time for the mixture to melt, 2 to 5 minutes.

12. Strain mixture through cheesecloth into a container and enjoy.

INFUSION WITH SLOW COOKER

When we think of a slow cooker, we think of a delicious juicy chicken, pot roast, or chili. It's also brilliant for making cannabutter or oil. It's an all-in-one place to infuse weed butter or weed oils while allowing you to keep the smell of weed at a minimum during the infusion process.

Time: *8½ hours, plus overnight to cool* 🌿 ***Appeal:*** *Mild taste* 🌿 ***Yield:*** *12 tablespoons*

WHAT YOU'LL NEED

1 cup water

8 ounces clarified butter (page 37), melted butter, oil, or fat

½ ounce decarboxylated cannabis material (page 36)

slow cooker

spoon

cheesecloth

knife

saucepan

storage container of choice

WHAT TO DO

1. Add water to the slow cooker.

2. Add the butter, oil, or fat directly into the slow cooker. Then, add the cannabis into the slow cooker and stir with a spoon until completely incorporated.

3. Put the lid onto slow cooker and let cook on low for 8 hours. After 8 hours have passed, the butter will have a glossy, glass-like top coat.

4. Secure a cheesecloth over your preferred storage container and strain the butter.

5. Be sure that the weed butter is completely cool before placing it into the freezer. Leave it overnight in a freezer-safe container.

6. Take the weed butter out of the freezer. With a knife, scrape the outside border, allowing you to pop out the entire piece. If it breaks, no worries; just be gentle. Flip over each piece to reveal and remove any excess moisture. The best way to do this is by either patting the butter with a paper towel or clean dish cloth, or by scraping with a knife.

7. In a saucepan over medium-low heat, slowly melt the moisture-free weed butter until liquefied, but not too hot.

8. Return the butter to a container to refrigerate or freeze for later use.

INFUSION WITH SOUS VIDE CIRCULATOR

I'm a little late to the game, but sous vide is one of my favorite infusion methods. Clean, simple, with little dirty work. I was introduced to sous vide–style cooking last year by the cutest couple from Seattle, who not only have exquisite taste for gastronomy and its culture, but also know the joys of mellowing out with cannabis-infused food. They gave me a Joule sous vide circulator from their company ChefSteps and I was hooked. And it was hands-down the most futuristic experience I'd ever had with cooking. This is the perfect setup if you're looking to infuse your weed butter, fat, or oil with garlic or other herbs.

__Time:__ 4 to 5 hours ✽ __Appeal:__ Easy cleanup ✽ __Yield:__ 12 tablespoons

WHAT YOU'LL NEED

8 ounces clarified butter (page 37), melted butter, oil, or fat

20-ounce jar or plastic bag

water

½ ounce decarboxylated cannabis material (page 36)

sous vide circulator

large pot

cheesecloth

storage container of choice

WHAT TO DO

1. Dice your butter into large squares and place it into a 20-ounce glass jar or a high-quality sealable plastic bag.

2. Add about 6 inches of water to your pot, making sure your sous vide tool is fully submerged in the water bath. If using a mason jar, close it tightly but not too tight, or your jar may burst into the water.

3. Set your sous vide circulator to 185°F and place your jar or bag into the water.

4. When you notice the butter melt, after 2 to 5 minutes, open the jar or bag, add your weed on top of the butter, reseal, and place back into the water.

5. Let your butter or oil infuse for 4 hours.

6. Secure a cheesecloth over your preferred storage container and strain the butter. Seal and store, or use immediately.

If you don't have a sous vide, use all the same steps, replacing a sous vide circulator with a slow cooker bath set to low for 6 hours.

INFUSION ON THE STOVETOP

If you have weed, butter, time, and a kitchen, you can make weed butter with this method. When it comes to ease, the stovetop infusion method is supreme. Perfect for folks who don't have a lot of extra money to spend on materials but still want good relief from cannabutter. Grab some butter, weed, and a pot, and let's get started.

Time: 4½ hours ✿ *Appeal:* Simplicity ✿ *Yield:* 12 tablespoons

WHAT YOU'LL NEED

½ cup water

8 ounces clarified butter (page 37), melted butter, oil, or fat

½ ounce decarboxylated cannabis material (page 36)

medium saucepan

wooden spoon

thermometer, optional

cheesecloth and/or metal strainer

WHAT TO DO

1. In a medium saucepan on very low heat, add the water and butter.

2. When the butter is melted, add the decarboxylated cannabis material. Mix well with a wooden spoon and cover with lid.

3. Let mixture gently simmer for 4 hours. Stir every half hour to make sure your butter isn't burning. If you have a thermometer, check to make sure the temperature doesn't reach above 180°F.

4. After 4 hours, strain with a cheesecloth or metal strainer into a container. Let the butter cool to room temperature. Use immediately or keep in refrigerator or freezer.

BACON CANNA-GREASE

This might be the most exciting thing that you're ever going to do with bacon. Which is hard to believe, because all things bacon-related are pretty damn exciting—so much so that there's a rare cult-like type of veganism and vegetarianism that makes an exception for bacon. Whoa.

This infusion process sort of entails two steps. But I promise, it's easy and worth it, because each involves you eating bacon in some form. You can use bacon canna-grease to roast potatoes, bake cornbread, cook mac and cheese, or make just about anything your fatty little heart desires. This can keep up to about one month in the refrigerator, or three months in the freezer.

Time: 20 minutes ☆ *Potency per serving: 1.5 mg per tablespoon of grease/1 to 5 mg per slice* ☆ *Yield: 5 to 8 tablespoons of canna-grease; 8 to 14 slices*

WHAT YOU'LL NEED

1 packet (8 to 14 pieces) thick-cut bacon

¼ ounce decarboxylated cannabis material (page 36)

oven

cookie sheet

mortar and pestle

salt shaker

glass jar or container

WHAT TO DO

1. Preheat your oven to 275°F and lay the bacon out on a cookie sheet.

2. Grind the decarboxylated weed into a fine powder with a mortar and pestle. Once it's in powder form, put into a salt shaker or some sort of container that allows you to evenly shake out the weed.

3. Evenly sprinkle about half of the weed onto your pieces of bacon. Bake for 10 minutes, and flip over to sprinkle the remaining cannabis material onto the other sides of bacon. Bake for another 10 minutes.

4. Once your pan has cooled, strain the bacon, allowing the grease to collect in the pan. Strain the fat into a glass jar or container.

Suggested Additional Infusion Herbs and Roots

When infusing weed, especially with the slow cooker and sous vide method, you can add an herb or root of choice if you're looking for some added flavor profiles. Here are a few I like to include during infusion (individually, or paired to your liking).

- Basil
- Cilantro
- Chives
- Garlic
- Ginger
- Mint
- Oregano
- Peppercorns
- Turmeric

Simply add a desired amount of herbs or roots to your butter before you begin the infusion process, and strain them out when you strain the weed.

Chapter *Four*
CANNABUTTERS AND OILS

Everybody's got choices when it comes to cooking. However, the flavor and smoking point of your oil means a lot. Coming from a West African background, I like to stick to mostly coconut or sunflower oil in the kitchen. When it comes to Italian foods and some sauces, olive oil is best. And when you want that buttery biscuit, you better use butter (or lard, if you're from the South). Here, I break down the many uses of my favorite cooking oils and what to choose when incorporating weed into your infusion or meal.

Classic Cannabutter

Butter has a bad rap and weed butter has swooped in to save its name. Despite having been demonized in the past, butter (especially from grass-fed cows) is actually pretty healthy. Cannabutter, a.k.a. weed butter, can go with almost everything, but I find that it complements baked goods, pastas, and rice dishes the best. Use a little or as much as you want to get the kind of relief or experience you desire.

Vegan Cannabutter, Margarine, and Ghee

Use vegan weed butter and margarine the same as you would regular butter. Add a slab onto pancakes, or even rice, for a creamier and more complex flavor. Ghee, essentially clarified butter (see page 37), is in a class of its own. It's been recently hyped up by Westerners for its nuttier flavor—this is after 30 years of shaming it for its high fat contents. Ghee, originally from the Indian subcontinent, loosely translates to "sprinkle" in Sanskrit. So sprinkle, or spread, it on anything you want, or anything that calls for butter. And since ghee separates milk from fat, it's essentially lactose-free, making it better than butter if you have to avoid dairy products.

Cannabis-Infused Sunflower, Grapeseed, and Canola Oils

Sunflower oil is the high-heat priestess, with a super-high smoking point of 440°F. It's followed by grapeseed oil at 420°F (this is a coincidence), and canola at a cool 400°F—which isn't cool at all. These types of oils are perfect to use for stir fries and fried dishes. Sunflower oil contains a small amount of pollen, which boosts its nutritional and THC-binding qualities.

Cannabis-Infused Coconut Oil

I love coconut oil. I use it topically on my skin and I cook with it. With nearly 86 percent of it containing healthy saturated fats, it's both a healthy and vegan option. Coconut oil has a burning point of about 350°F, so feel free to sauté with it, but do not fry with it. Swap it for butter in sweet or savory dishes. It's great for soups, stews, and baking.

Cannabis-Infused Avocado Seed Oil

Like the oil of the gods, goddesses, and other deities, avocado seed oil cures everything with a luxurious edge. Drizzle cannabis-infused avocado oil on toast, rice, or fish. Use it on your face for sun damage, psoriasis, or acne. Slather it on your hair as a hot-oil treatment to deeply moisturize afros and locks. Unrefined, cold-pressed, extra-virgin avocado oil is best, as it's known to be packed with vitamins B and C and to contribute to the prevention of heart disease and cancer.

Cannabis-Infused Olive Oil

Olive oil has made its way into our hearts and bellies for centuries. It's the best canna oil for salad dressings, drizzling over soups (hot and cold), prepared food, pasta, sauces, or even your skin. It's exceptionally high in oleic acid, which is known to burn fat, assist with weight loss, and help reduce high blood pressure. Olive oil also contains many antioxidants, including vitamin E, carotenoids, and oleuropein.

Chapter Five

WAKE AND BAKE: LOW-DOSE BREAKFASTS

MORNING MEDICATED FRUIT BOWL

I'm one of those people who needs a couple hours in the morning before diving into a big breakfast. I recall dreadful moments as a child where I had to eat toast and oatmeal with a glass each of orange juice and milk in the morning. As I write this, I imagine all of those things curdling inside of my stomach. While I'm lucky to have been fed before school, it's made me become a grown woman who prefers a breakfast that is light, yet nutritious. The added wake and bake benefit doesn't hurt either. This medicated fruit bowl is healthy, pretty, and easy to make. Use any berries you'd like, such as strawberries, blueberries, raspberries, or blackberries. What's more, it's packed with enough energy to keep you full and focused throughout the morning, with a healthy dose of THC to chill you the *bleep* out before tackling a potentially stressful day.

Time: 5 minutes ✦ *Potency per serving: 15 mg* ✦ *Yield: 2 servings*

WHAT YOU'LL NEED

1½ cups plain yogurt

1 teaspoon cannabis-infused coconut oil, or as desired

1 tablespoon chia seeds, nuts, or granola

1 handful berries

½ banana, sliced, optional

WHAT TO DO

1. Spoon out your yogurt into a bowl, mason jar, or large cup. Add your desired amount of cannabis-infused coconut oil.

2. Whip gently with a spoon or fork until evenly mixed. Mix in any seeds, nuts, or granola.

3. Top with berries and banana, if using, and enjoy!

EASY CHEESE CANNABIS SPINACH FRITTATA

The word "frittata" always seems fancy, but really, it's just a large omelet that you never have to flip—or is it a quiche without a pie crust? Either way, it's one of the simplest breakfast dishes that can "wow" anyone. Feel free to stick to the recipe and use the ingredients below, or add whatever vegetables or cheeses that are already hanging out in your refrigerator—I used queso Oaxaca in this recipe. Into something more meaty? Add bacon, leftover sausage, or chorizo. You literally can't really go wrong with a frittata.

Time: 25 minutes ⚘ *Potency per serving:* 3 mg ⚘ *Yield:* 5 servings

WHAT YOU'LL NEED

½ medium onion, diced

2 cloves garlic, minced

2 tablespoons olive oil

1 cup spinach or other leafy greens

5 eggs

½ cup milk, dairy or nondairy

1 small tomato, sliced

1 teaspoon cannabutter or cannabis-infused olive oil

½ cup grated melting cheese

salt and black pepper, to taste

WHAT TO DO

1. In a medium pan over medium heat, sauté the onion and garlic in olive oil for 5 minutes, letting them cook until transparent and your kitchen smells like heaven.

2. Add cannabutter or cannabis-infused olive oil and spinach or other green leafy vegetables and cook for 1 to 2 minutes.

3. Whisk the eggs with milk and pour evenly over the veggies.

4. Spread the cheese over the eggs like it's a pizza, placing the sliced tomatoes similarly.

5. Cover the eggs with a lid or plate for 5 to 10 minutes on low heat, or longer if you like your eggs extra crispy at the bottom. The eggs will puff up, signifying that they're done.

6. Remove the lid, slice into six slices, and enjoy!

SIMPLE STONEY HASH BROWNS

Everyone loves hash browns (I hope you're not the exception), but not everyone knows how easy they are to make from scratch. This can be dangerous, because once you do, you're going to have them all the time. Hash browns are the staple comfort breakfast food. Luckily, because these are dosed with cannabis, you might only have them on those slow and lazy Sunday mornings.

Time: 30 minutes ✾ *Potency per serving:* 7.25 mg ✾ *Yield:* 2 servings

WHAT YOU'LL NEED

1 pound (about 3 large) potatoes

3 tablespoons extra-virgin olive oil

1 teaspoon cannabis-infused olive oil or cannabutter

salt and black pepper, to taste

WHAT TO DO

1. Shred the potatoes with a cheese grater. Be careful with your fingers. The bigger the potatoes you use, the better. Once grated, season with salt and pepper, to taste.

2. Add the olive oil and cannabis-infused olive oil or cannabutter to a medium pan or skillet over medium heat.

3. Add the shredded potatoes evenly and let them cook until you see the bottom start to become crisp, about 8 minutes.

4. Flip with a spatula. (The skillet should be greasy enough for you to do a pan flip if you wanted—trust me!)

5. Let cook for about 5 minutes, until the hash browns have reached preferred crispiness.

FLUFFY MEDICATED BLUEBERRY MINI-CAKES

I know what you're thinking—really Mennlay, weed in pancakes? Yes and let me tell you why. These fluffy, buttery, and maybe a little too rich pancakes will be a weekend game changer. These are not everyday pancakes so save it for a special Saturday homemade brunch with your best friends. Or maybe a sleepy Saturday treat after a long week of work. Just try them and you'll see what I'm talking about. I made a blueberry sauce with the leftover blueberries, but feel free to keep it old school with maple syrup or agave nectar.

Time: 30 minutes ❋ *Potency per serving:* 2.5 mg per pancake ❋ *Yield:* 12 pancakes

WHAT YOU'LL NEED

2 cups flour

1½ teaspoons baking powder

¼ teaspoon baking soda

¼ cup sugar

1 teaspoon salt

1 teaspoon butter, plus more for greasing

2 teaspoons cannabutter or cannabis-infused canola oil

4 eggs

2 cups cream or yogurt

2 cups fresh blueberries

WHAT TO DO

1. In a medium bowl, mix together the flour, baking powder, baking soda, sugar, and salt.

2. In a small saucepan, melt 1 teaspoon of plain butter plus the cannabutter or cannabis-infused canola oil over low heat just until they become a liquid, not letting them boil.

3. Add the melted butter to the dry ingredients. Gently mix with a spatula.

4. Add the eggs and cream or yogurt, and beat gently until the mixture is free of clumps. The batter should be wet, but not too watery.

5. Add half of the blueberries and gently mix, being sure to not crush them.

6. Place a large skillet over medium heat and grease with a generous amount of butter so the pancakes cook without sticking.

7. Using an ice cream scoop or measuring cup with a spout, pour out your disks of pancakes. They should be 2 to 3 inches in diameter.

8. Cook until you see small bubbles/holes, about 2 minutes, then flip. Cook for another 2 minutes. Continue until batter is done.

9. To make the blueberry sauce, mix the remaining blueberries with water and heat in a saucepan until a sauce thickens, about 5 minutes. Serve hot.

ELEVATED AVOCADO TOAST

Before you roll your eyes at this millennial snack, know that I'm an elder millennial who lives in Mexico—how could I not add this recipe into the mix? Enjoy as a breakfast or snack that is packed with vitamins B and C and all the good fats, and it has a nice drizzle of cannabis avocado or olive oil for extra goodness. This is a perfect edible for on the go, a nice mellow morning vibe, or a snack to help with any ailments or pain from the day.

Time: 3 minutes ✹ *Potency per serving:* 14.5 mg ✹ *Yield:* 1 serving

WHAT YOU'LL NEED

1 avocado

2 slices of bread, toasted

1 teaspoon cannabis-infused olive oil

2 cherry tomatoes, halved, optional

1 lime, halved

salt and black pepper, to taste

WHAT TO DO

1. Cut the avocado in half and scoop the flesh onto the slices of toasted bread. Season with salt and black pepper, to taste.

2. Drizzle cannabis-infused olive oil on each slice. Add cherry tomatoes, if desired. Squeeze a little lime on top of that for an added antioxidant boost.

Some people like to get fancy with the avocado design. I don't, because this toast goes into my mouth basically as soon as I'm done spearing the avocado on the bread. Feel free to make it cute by slicing and dicing a design onto your toast. I won't stop you.

Chapter Six

SAUCES, SPREADS, AND DRESSINGS

CANNA-OIL CHOCOLATE HAZELNUT SPREAD

This is everything. I mean, it's Nutella with weed! Eat a spoonful to curb your stoned sweet tooth. Spread it on toast, add it to a smoothie, or use it as a frosting on cake, brownies. Melt it on strawberries, blackberries, bananas—any fruit of choice. This is super easy to make, which means you get to put it in your mouth that much sooner.

Time: 2 minutes ✹ *Potency per tablespoon:* 1 mg ✹ *Yield:* 24 tablespoons (1½ cups)

WHAT YOU'LL NEED

1 (375-gram) jar of Nutella or another store-bought chocolate hazelnut spread

2 tablespoons cannabutter or cannabis-infused coconut oil

WHAT TO DO

Add the cannabis-infused coconut oil or weed butter to Nutella. Mix well by hand. Serve and enjoy.

PHILLY JALAPEÑO CREMA

I have a friend name Philip, but his nickname is Philly. Philly always makes the most delicious dishes topped with this vegan crema sauce. Two years ago, he moved to Tulum with his partner and one night, after many mescals, he finally gave me the recipe. Use as a dip for chips, fries, or as a spread for burgers and sandwiches. Keep in the refrigerator for up to one week.

Time: 20 minutes ❧ *Potency per recipe:* 14.5 mg ❧ *Yield:* 2 cups

WHAT YOU'LL NEED

6 jalapeños

½ bunch of cilantro

1 tablespoon olive oil

1 teaspoon cannabis-infused olive oil

1 tablespoon cumin

pinch of cayenne

3 to 5 cloves garlic, minced

salt and black pepper, to taste

WHAT TO DO

1. Add the jalapeños to a small saucepan. Fill with just enough water to cover. Bring the water to a boil, then lower to a simmer. Cook for about 15 minutes. Drain.

2. In a blender, add the boiled jalapeños, cilantro, both oils, cumin, cayenne, garlic, salt, and pepper, and blend until it reaches a thick but creamy consistency. Add more water if necessary.

ELEVATED TOMATO SAUCE

Tomato sauce should be simple—I mean, it's just tomatoes. Of course, in this recipe, I add a few extra ingredients, like garlic, pepper flakes, and cannabutter. The good thing about this sauce is that you're welcome to use as little or as many of the extras I added. The legs of this sauce are the tomatoes (canned tomatoes are fine), salt, and cannabutter. The rest is up to you! Serve as a pizza sauce, a dip for breadsticks, a simple pasta sauce, or base for tomato soup.

Time: *1 hour* ✹ **Potency per recipe:** *14.5 mg* ✹ **Yield:** *3 cups*

WHAT YOU'LL NEED

2 cups chopped tomatoes

1 teaspoon cannabutter

2 tablespoons butter

½ teaspoon sugar

2 cloves garlic

1 tablespoon salt

1 tablespoon crushed black pepper

1 tablespoon red pepper flakes

1 cup shredded Parmesan cheese

WHAT DO TO

1. Add all ingredients to a large saucepan and bring to a simmer on low heat. Be sure to not let the butter burn too fast.

2. Let simmer, covered, for 45 minutes to an hour, stirring and smashing tomatoes and garlic every 15 minutes. I prefer to keep mine chunky and rustic. If you fancy a pureed consistency, once cooled, blend the sauce with a blender or a food processor.

NUTTY VEGAN CHIPOTLE AIOLI

I put this on everything. I use it as a dip for sweet potato fries or strips of fried chicken, and as a spread for sandwiches. What's more, it's vegan, creamy, full of flavor, and lasts for months. I've found that buying 7-ounce can of chipotle in adobo sauce is a lifesaver. I prefer the La Costeña brand. Just put it in a sealed container and pop it in the refrigerator—good luck not finishing it all in one sitting.

Time: *10 minutes, plus time to soak*
Potency per recipe: *14.5 mg* **Yield:** *1 cup*

WHAT YOU'LL NEED

1 cup raw cashews

½ cup soy, almond, or coconut milk

2 to 3 chipotle peppers

1 teaspoon adobo sauce

1 small clove garlic

2 tablespoons lime juice

1 teaspoon agave nectar or raw sugar

1 teaspoon cannabis-infused avocado seed oil

salt, to taste

WHAT TO DO

1. At least one hour up to one night before, soak your cashews in a bowl of hot water with a pinch of salt; you can either leave the soaking nuts on your counter or refrigerate. Strain cashews and store covered in the refrigerator until ready to blend.

2. In a blender, add the soaked cashews, milk, peppers, adobo sauce, and garlic, and pulse until smooth.

3. Add the lime, sugar, cannabis-infused oil, and a pinch of salt.

4. Blend until smooth, using a wooden spoon to remove any chunks that might not be blending.

5. Store in the refrigerator for up to one week.

CLASSIC WEED BALSAMIC VINAIGRETTE

I honestly don't remember the last time I bought salad dressing. It's not because I'm a domestic goddess—okay maybe a little. It's mostly because making salad dressing at home is much easier and more inexpensive, and you know exactly what you're putting into it. A classic vinaigrette is a perfect match for the deep and earthy profile of a cannabis-infused olive oil. This recipe for balsamic vinaigrette comes from a great friend, author, and home cook, David Lida. Use at your discretion with any salad and use bread to soak up whatever is left on your plate.

Time: 15 minutes ✹ *Potency per recipe:* 30 mg ✹ *Yield:* 1 cup

WHAT YOU'LL NEED
2 cloves garlic, finely chopped

1 teaspoon salt

1 teaspoon ground pepper

1 teaspoon Dijon mustard

1 teaspoon cannabis-infused olive oil

4 tablespoons olive oil

3 tablespoons balsamic vinegar

WHAT TO DO
In a dish, whisk together the garlic pieces, salt, pepper, Dijon, and cannabis-infused oil. Add the regular olive oil and vinegar and whisk to combine. Add more vinegar or oil to your taste.

GREEN GANJA DRESSING

Green Goddess dressing: originally created in San Francisco and now widely loved throughout the entire world. This simple pesto-like dressing is just as easy to make as it is to eat. I put it on everything—bread, salad, grilled chicken. Sometimes I eat spoonfuls of it when no one is watching. (Is that weird? Probably.) This recipe, which uses cannabis-infused olive oil, has a nice earthy taste. Cannabis-infused avocado seed oil works beautifully, too. You decide.

Time: 15 minutes ✷ *Potency per recipe:* 30 mg ✷ *Yield:* 2 cups

WHAT YOU'LL NEED

1½ cups plain yogurt

1½ packed cups basil leaves

¼ packed cup chives

2 cloves garlic

1 green onion, chopped

2 anchovy fillets, optional

1 teaspoon lime juice

1 lime, zested

1 tablespoon extra-virgin olive oil

2 teaspoons cannabis-infused olive oil

salt and pepper, to taste

WHAT TO DO

Add all the ingredients into a blender and purée. Add salt and black pepper to taste.

GUACAMOLE MÁGICO

Living both in Mexico and California, I know a good guacamole. The simpler, the better. If you have avocado you're basically set, because the rest, you'll likely have on hand. I like to eat my guac with plantain chips rather than tortilla chips because I'm still an African girl, but feel free to accompany it with whatever your stoner heart desires.

Time: 10 minutes 🌿 *Potency per recipe:* 14.5 mg 🌿 *Yield:* 2 cups

WHAT YOU'LL NEED

4 avocados, pitted

½ small onion, minced

½ jalapeño, minced

1 teaspoon salt

2 cloves garlic, minced

1 teaspoon cannabis-infused olive oil

fresh or dried cilantro, for garnish

WHAT TO DO

Scoop all the avocado flesh into a medium bowl. Add the remaining ingredients and mix with a spoon to reach your desired chunkiness. Garnish with cilantro.

Chapter Seven

MAINS AND SIDES

CUTE AND CHEESY MACARONI BAKE

Let me get real with you for a second. You can legit just use a box of really yummy organic macaroni and cheese, mix some weed butter in it, and call it a chill night. But mac and cheese isn't hard to make. For better or worse, being a black girl raised in the United States has stereotyped me into not only loving this dish, but also knowing how to make it from scratch. What black Thanksgiving have you ever been to that doesn't have homemade macaroni and cheese? What funeral or wake? What really good cookout (well, maybe that gets switched for macaroni salad but you get my point). I dare you to make this at your next family event. And please, for legal reasons and for just plain being a good person, make sure everyone knows that there's weed in this dish. Adults only. Use whatever type of cheddar cheese you like best for this recipe—mild, regular, or sharp.

Time: 45 minutes ❋ *Potency per serving: 3.75 mg* ❋ *Yield: 4 servings*

WHAT YOU'LL NEED

2 cups dry macaroni pasta

2 tablespoons flour

½ cup cream cheese

1 cup milk

1 tablespoon butter, room temperature

1 teaspoon cannabutter, room temperature

½ teaspoon salt

½ teaspoon freshly ground black pepper

pinch red pepper flakes

3 cloves garlic, minced

1½ cups shredded white cheddar cheese, divided

WHAT TO DO

1. Preheat the oven to 375°F.

2. In a medium pot, boil water. Once boiling, add the macaroni.

3. Cook pasta on medium-high heat for 7 to 10 minutes, or until al dente, then strain.

4. Put strained pasta into a large mixing bowl, then add the flour, cream cheese, milk, butters, salt, pepper, red pepper flakes, garlic, and half of the cheddar. Mix well to combine.

5. Transfer the pasta mixture into four individual oven-safe ramekins or, if you'd prefer, an oven-safe baking dish. Then, add the remaining cheddar on top.

6. Bake for 20 minutes until the cheese is bubbly and slightly browned.

7. Let sit for 5 minutes to cool before serving.

WEST AFRICAN FRIED CHICKEN

Fried chicken is more of an American staple than it is African. Turns out most Southern staples are a mix of African, Indigenous, and European cuisines, which makes total sense when we think about the history of the United States and its foundations. But growing up in a West African household in the 1980s meant that on occasion, my mother would treat us to "American" cuisine. Mostly, we ate traditional West African dishes like cassava leaf and rice, jollof rice, fufu, and soup. So when my sweet mother treated us girls to fried chicken, she put her take on it—spicy and savory, with a hint of sweet, and lots of crunchiness. I'm super excited to share with you my take on my mama's West African fried chicken recipe, with a hint of cannabis of course. You can substitute cayenne chili powder for the chopped peppers if you don't have any on hand. This recipe is a low dose, meant for you to enjoy more than one piece without getting too blazed. You're welcome.

Time: *50 minutes, plus time to marinate* ✲ ***Potency per piece:*** *3.75 mg* ✲ ***Yield:*** *8 pieces*

WHAT YOU'LL NEED

3 pounds (8 mixed pieces) chicken

2 teaspoons cannabis-infused grapeseed oil

2 teaspoons salt

2 teaspoons black pepper

2 large cloves garlic, finely chopped

1 to 2 tablespoons chopped serrano or jalapeño peppers

1 teaspoon honey

1 egg

½ cup milk

2 cups flour

1 tablespoon cornmeal (grits or polenta)

vegetable oil, for frying

WHAT TO DO

1. Clean the chicken and pat dry, then place it in a large bowl. Add the cannabis-infused grapeseed oil into the bowl. Stir with a wooden spoon or wooden spatula to make sure the oil coats the chicken evenly. This will ensure the most accurate dose per piece.

2. Add salt, black pepper, garlic, hot peppers, and honey, continuing to stir until the chicken is coated evenly.

3. Place chicken in the refrigerator for at least 10 minutes to overnight.

4. In a medium bowl, whisk the egg and milk together. In a separate bowl, sift the flour and cornmeal together.

5. Remove the marinated chicken from refrigerator.

6. In a deep frying pan, add about 1 inch of vegetable oil. Turn the burner up to medium-high heat. Allow the oil to heat up for 1 or 2 minutes. To test the heat, sprinkle a tiny grain of your flour mixture. If it pops up to surface, it's ready for your chicken.

7. Dip each piece of chicken into the whisked egg and milk mixture, then into the flour. Gently pat the flour onto the chicken so that it sticks and coats each piece. Gently place the chicken pieces into the frying pan. Make sure to leave a little space in between each piece to keep them from sticking together while frying.

8. With tongs or a large metal spoon, turn each piece every 5 minutes for about 20 minutes total, until the pieces are perfectly brown. If it seems like the chicken is cooking too fast or spattering too much oil, turn the burner down to medium.

9. Once cooked, place the chicken onto a couple sheets of wax paper or paper towels. Let rest for a couple minutes and then serve!

GARLIC-CRUNCH SWEET POTATO FRIES

Do you know someone who doesn't like fries? I don't. And what's better than fries? Sweet potato fries! They're ingenious, taste waaaaay better than regular potato fries, and are much better for you. (I like to keep on some of the skin.) They have obscene amounts of potassium, vitamin C, fiber, and calcium, and are known by some health gurus to help fight cancer because of their antioxidant properties. Sweet potatoes help lower blood sugar, despite being sweet. They're also a great, inexpensive baby food. Just bake in the oven in aluminum foil and mash up for the baby. She'll love them! But this recipe is not for babies—it's just for fancy grown-ups at a weed-infused dinner.

Time: *45 minutes* ✿
Potency per serving: *3.75 mg* ✿ **Yield:** *4 servings*

WHAT YOU'LL NEED

3 medium sweet potatoes, peeled as desired, cut lengthwise into ½-inch strips

2 large cloves garlic, minced

pinch of coarse salt

1 teaspoon crushed black pepper

pinch of cayenne

4 tablespoons coconut oil

1 teaspoon cannabis-infused sunflower oil

WHAT TO DO

1. Preheat the oven to 400°F.

2. Place the potatoes in a baking dish, spreading them out evenly.

3. Mix in your spices and oils, making sure to coat the potatoes evenly. Bake for 45 minutes, until crispy. Mix halfway through the cooking time.

CHEESY FLATBREAD PIZZAS

Perhaps flatbread is pizza to you, but to me, it's an opportunity to make pizza's more chill, less needy sister. Not that there's anything wrong with being needy. Let's just say that I'm a major fangirl of flatbread. It's easy to make because you don't have to wait around all day for the dough to rise. You can eat it plain or put just about anything on it. I went the classic route of vegetables and melty cheese to make it more pizza like, but be adventurous if you'd like. Add slices of pear, chunks of blue cheese, and arugula. Get fancy and top it with thin shaves of prosciutto and Parmesan on a bed of caramelized onions. Or you can be lazy and only add salt, honey, dried herbs, and drizzles of cannabis-infused olive oil. It does not matter what you do to this flatbread; it is going to gently rock your world.

Time: 45 minutes ✹ *Potency per serving:* 3.75 mg ✹ *Yield:* 8 servings

WHAT YOU'LL NEED

For the flatbread:

1¾ cups flour

1 teaspoon baking powder

pinch of coarse salt

3 tablespoons olive oil

2 teaspoons cannabis-infused olive oil

½ cup water

dried herbs of choice, optional

For the topping:

½ cup mozzarella

handful of cherry tomatoes

1 large zucchini, sliced

½ red onion, thinly sliced

pinch of oregano

pinch of salt

WHAT TO DO

1. Preheat your oven to 420°F.

2. In a large mixing bowl, add the flour, baking powder, and salt. Make a little hole and add your oils and water, slowly mixing with a spoon until it comes together.

3. Pick up the dough and knead a couple times. Add in desired herbs, if using. Roll out into 2 or 3 sections.

4. Place the dough sections onto a dry pizza or cookie sheet and place in the center rack of the oven for 3 to 5 minutes until it is about halfway golden.

5. Take the bread out of the oven and add toppings in your preferred order.

6. Place the dough back into oven for 10 minutes, lowering the temperature to 375°F. Keep an eye on it to be sure it cooks to your preference.

7. Let cool before removing onto a cutting board or pizza dish, and enjoy!

Alternatively, while making the flatbread, you can use 5 tablespoons of non-infused olive oil, and while topping the flatbread, use 2 tablespoons of Elevated Tomato Sauce (page 66) to get your buzz.

SUMMER SQUASH LASAGNA

Oh, lasagna! It's such an easy dish...unless you're one of those amazing Italian grandmothers who make all of their pastas from scratch. I think the only pasta I've ever tried to make from scratch was gnocchi. Though it was absolutely worth it, it took about 3 hours to make the entire dish. I mean, is it that serious? We're living in the future where if you're lucky enough, you can even cop a delicious, organic, locally-made, frozen lasagna. As you already know, I don't judge about those things. So if you want to just grab one of them and brush 2 teaspoons of weed butter or cannabis-infused olive oil on top of it, do it! Note that the potency for this dish is measured without the Elevated Tomato Sauce.

Time: *1½ hours* ❋ ***Potency per serving:*** *5 mg* ❋ ***Yield:*** *6 servings*

WHAT YOU'LL NEED

3 cups shredded mozzarella

½ cup grated Parmesan cheese

½ cup ricotta

1 egg

1 box (about 16 sheets) lasagna pasta

4 large cloves garlic, minced

2 medium zucchinis, sliced

1 red onion, finely sliced

¾ cup olive oil

1½ cups white wine

4 cups store-bought tomato sauce or Elevated Tomato Sauce (page 66)

2 teaspoons cannabis-infused olive oil

1 teaspoon herbs de Provence

salt and black pepper, to taste

WHAT TO DO

1. Preheat the oven to 350°F.

2. In a large bowl, mix cheeses, salt, pepper, and egg with a wooden spoon. Set aside.

3. In a separate bowl, let the pasta soak in hot water for 20 minutes.

4. In a medium saucepan over high heat, sauté garlic, zucchinis, onion, olive oil, and white wine for 5 to 10 minutes until liquid is reduced. Set aside.

5. In a lightly greased baking dish, first place layers of lasagna followed by tomato sauce, cheese mixture, and sautéed veggies. Continue and repeat this layering process, ending with lasagna pasta.

6. Brush cannabis-infused olive oil on the last layer of pasta, then add tomato sauce and cheese on top. Sprinkle herbs de Provence on top for color and taste.

7. Cover the lasagna with foil and bake in oven for 40 minutes, until bubbly. Remove the foil and bake for another 10 to 15 minutes until it reaches desired amount of crispy yummy cheesiness.

8. Let cool for 5 to 10 minutes before serving.

If using a frozen store-bought lasagna, follow oven reheating directions. Take out five minutes prior to finishing, evenly brush on weed olive oil, and place back in the oven for remaining minutes. Take out, let cool, and serve.

CHACAHUA COCONUT BEANS AND RICE

You can't tell from the photo, but there's a lot of juiciness on that plate of beans and rice. I think bean juice should be used more as a sauce, or salsa, base more often. An ingenious technique in Mexican cuisine is to blend the beans and juice and use as a spread. This recipe is inspired by one of my favorite places in Mexico, Chacahua, nestled on a lagoon on the coast of Oaxaca—a land known for its exotic birds, glowing bioluminescence, and silent settlement of freed slaves. The people of Chacahua, like most freed African communities in the late twentieth century, settled in a remote location in hopes of curating a future of their own and avoiding scrutiny for being black in Mexico. I like to eat my beans and rice accompanied by lightly breaded white fish, but it's flavorful enough to eat on its own.

Time: 3 hours 🌿 *Potency per serving:* 5 to 7.5 mg 🌿 *Yield:* 4 to 6 servings

WHAT YOU'LL NEED

For the beans

1½ cups black beans

2 bay leaves

3 cloves garlic, minced

1 medium onion, finely chopped

½ cup finely chopped cilantro

1 fresh serrano pepper, deseeded and minced

1 bell pepper, finely chopped

1 teaspoon fresh thyme leaves, or ½ teaspoon dried thyme

salt and black pepper, to taste

1 teaspoon cannabis-infused coconut oil

2 tablespoons extra-virgin olive oil

For the rice

1½ cups white rice

3 cups water

1 can coconut milk

1 teaspoon cannabis-infused coconut oil

salt, to taste

WHAT TO DO

1. In a large pot, add the beans, bay leaves, and enough water to cover the beans by an inch. Bring to a boil.

2. After 20 minutes, turn down to a strong and steady simmer and add the garlic, onion, cilantro, and serrano and bell peppers, thyme, salt, and pepper. Cook for about 3 hours, stirring and adding more water when necessary.

3. Within the last hour of cooking your beans, add the cannabis-infused coconut oil, olive oil.

4. Meanwhile, rinse the rice. Add the rice to a medium pot and top with the water. Bring to a boil.

5. Turn the heat to a low simmer and add the coconut milk, cannabis-infused coconut oil, and a few pinches of salt. Let cook for 15 to 20 minutes.

6. Serve by spooning beans over rice, or both on the side with fried chicken, fish, or grilled veggies.

SIMPLE GANJA GRILLED ASPARAGUS

Other than what it does to your urine, asparagus is my all-time favorite green. It's hearty, has a beautiful color, and is perfectly crunchy—if you don't overcook it. Fun fact: Like the cannabis plant, asparagus plants also grow with sexual differences. As in, there are female and male plants. But most of the ones we eat are male.

Time: 10 minutes ☘ *Potency per serving: 7.5 mg* ☘ *Yield: 4 servings*

WHAT YOU'LL NEED
2 cloves garlic, chopped, optional

2 teaspoons cannabis-infused olive oil

3 tablespoons olive oil

1 bunch thin asparagus (about 40 spears)

WHAT TO DO
1. To a large saucepan over high heat, add the garlic, if using, and oils, and sauté until the garlic begins to look transparent.

2. Add the asparagus and cook for 4 to 5 minutes, turning over frequently, until cooked to desired tenderness.

SMOOTH AND SAVORY SHRIMP AND GRITS

Shrimp and grits seem much more difficult to make but it's just sautéed shrimps in a sweet and savory tomato medley over grits. But do believe the hype, because it's pretty damn delicious. If you don't eat seafood or meat, swap out shrimp for cauliflower florets, bell peppers, and zucchini. If you're feeling like you want to step up the meat action a notch, add spicy sausage for a complex and gratifying flavor. I started making this several years ago when I lived in Oakland, California, where there's this divine place called Brown Sugar Kitchen. After making a reservation early enough to get a table, I ordered their shrimp and grits and would crave it every weekend thereafter. Like the frugal lady I am, I decided to try to make it myself one weekend. And it was easy! Years later, I thought it could be a nice stony Sunday brunch staple, and here we are today.

Time: 1 hour 🌿 *Potency per serving:* 7.5 mg 🌿 *Yield:* 4 servings

WHAT YOU'LL NEED

1½ pounds tiger shrimp, cleaned and deveined

1 teaspoon cayenne pepper

2 cups water

1 cup corn grits

½ cup milk, plus more as needed

¾ stick butter, divided

1 cup shredded sharp cheddar cheese

2 teaspoons cannabutter or cannabis-infused coconut oil

2 to 3 cloves garlic, chopped

½ red onion, chopped

1 cup cherry tomatoes

1 bunch of green onions, chopped

¼ cup white wine or rice wine vinegar

cilantro, for garnish

hot sauce, to serve

salt and black pepper, to taste

WHAT TO DO

1. In a medium bowl, mix the shrimp with cayenne, salt, and pepper.

2. In a saucepan, bring two cups of water to a soft boil and add the grits. Once boiling, lower the heat to a low simmer. Add salt, pepper, milk, and ½ stick of butter, and stir frequently. Sprinkle in shredded cheese while continuing to stir to avoid clumping. Add more milk or water if necessary until grits come to a creamy yet thick consistency, about 10 minutes. Remove from heat and cover with lid.

3. To a sauté pan over high heat, add the cannabutter or cannabis-infused coconut oil along with the remaining butter. Add the garlic, red onion, tomatoes, and green onions, and sauté for about 10 minutes.

4. Add white wine or rice wine vinegar and gently smash the cherry tomatoes and garlic. Let cook for 2 to 3 minutes and add the shrimp. Turn up to a high heat and let the shrimp flash fry for about 1 minute on each side.

5. Once the shrimp turns pale pink, mix until the tomatoes, wine, and shrimp produce a nice thin sauce, 3 to 5 minutes.

6. Serve over grits, garnished with cilantro. Enjoy with a couple splashes of your favorite hot sauce.

CANNABIS-INFUSED MEXICAN STREET CORN (ESQUITES)

I know my Mexican friends are either going to laugh at or love this. Yet, alas, here is my new favorite weed-infused esquites. If you've ever visited Mexico or been anywhere with a large Mexican community, you already know about the street food. What I love the most about esquites is that it's a snack that you can take with you on your way out for errands or coming back from errands to keep your hanger at bay—yes, hanger, that's hunger and anger combined. This recipe is key for keeping your chill during those tightly scheduled days in the summer. Add it as a juicy and flavorful side for a Thanksgiving or a chill dinner with friends. Use a crumbly Mexican cheese like queso fresco, anejo, cotija, or manchego.

Time: 20 minutes ✺ *Potency per serving:* 3.75 mg ✺ *Yield:* 4 servings

WHAT YOU'LL NEED

3 cups corn (about 4 ears, shucked and kernels removed from cob)

¼ cup vegetable stock

1 teaspoon cannabutter

1 teaspoon butter

1 clove garlic, minced

1 teaspoon dried oregano

½ cup grated Mexican cheese, divided

½ serrano pepper, deseeded and finely chopped

cayenne pepper, to taste

squeeze of lime

1 heaping tablespoon mayonnaise, optional

salt and black pepper, to taste

cilantro, to garnish, optional

WHAT TO DO

1. Fill a large, steep-sided pan with 1 or 2 inches of water and bring to boil. Add the corn and let come up to boil again before reducing the heat to low. Cover the pan with a lid. Steam for about 10 minutes or until desired tenderness.

2. In a saucepan over medium heat, add vegetable stock, weed butter, regular butter, garlic, corn, oregano, if using, salt, pepper, and one quarter of the cheese. Let softly boil until some of the liquid reduces. Cook for about 5 to 10 minutes, stirring a couple times, being sure to not let all of the juices evaporate.

3. Serve with the remaining cheese, a couple dashes of cayenne, a squeeze of lime, and mayo, if using. Garnish with cilantro.

MENNLAY'S MEDICATED FRIED PLANTAINS

One of the best treats growing up in a West African household are plantains. Here in Mexico they are called platanos maduros (which means ripe plantains). They are an international treat, found in Jamaica, Peru, East Africa, and even Southeast Asia. But my favorite way is the way my mother cooks them. You know plantains are ripe when they are almost black—that's the type you need for this recipe.

Time: 20 minutes ✹ *Potency:* 5 mg ✹
Yield: 6 servings

WHAT YOU'LL NEED

4 ripe plantains

2 teaspoons cannabis-infused olive, coconut, canola, or vegetable oil

½ cup coconut oil or vegetable oil for frying

salt, to taste

crema, to serve

WHAT TO DO

1. Use a knife to slice the top and bottom end off each plantain, exposing the inside. Then slice the outer skin to easily peel back the plantain.

2. Once peeled, slice the plantains. I slice them at an angle to make the pieces a little larger. Feel free to slice to your preference.

3. In a large frying pan over medium to high heat, add your oils, making sure to mix the cannabis-infused oil evenly. Let the oils heat for about 1 minute.

4. Add each piece of plantain one by one so that they are not touching; sprinkle with salt. Turn over once golden, after about 5 to 10 minutes, and do the same for the next side. Remove to a paper towel or parchment paper until cool. Drizzle crema or put on the side for an optional dip.

*Chapter **Eight***
SWEETS

NUTTY POT BROWNIE BARS

Oh, the pot brownie. To many this is the most recognized, most classic edible. Can I tell you a little secret though? I'm not a huge chocolate fan. I know, I know! The truth is I just don't crave chocolate. What do I crave? Gummy bears. Before you write me off as an indecent human being, hear this—what I do like in a chocolate bar or brownie is a little crunch. And I loveeeeee chocolate when it's mixed with nuts or just about anything creamy. The cannabis-infused fat goes right into your favorite store-bought box of brownie mix, or you can mix it from scratch. With a nod to the original "Hashish Fudge" from Alice B. Toklas, this recipe calls for cashews to complement the earthy moisture from the weed butter, giving it a soft crunch.

Time: *45 minutes* ❧ **Potency per serving:** *4.8 mg* ❧ **Yield:** *12 servings*

WHAT YOU'LL NEED

1 (18-ounce) box brownie mix

3 eggs

2 cups milk

2 heaping tablespoons sour cream

4 teaspoons cannabutter

½ cup cocoa nibs or a handful of chocolate chips, optional

½ cup cashews or nuts of choice, optional

WHAT TO DO

1. Preheat the oven to 350°F.

2. Take the ingredients out of the box and start by adding the dry ingredients together in one mixing bowl.

3. In another bowl, add the eggs, milk, sour cream, and cannabutter. Slowly add in the dry ingredients.

4. If using nuts, pulse in a blender or food processor for 2 seconds and sprinkle into the brownie mix. Gently fold in the nuts and cocoa nibs or chocolate chips, if using.

5. Butter a 9 x 9-inch square baking pan, then fill until about ¾ full. If using a shallow baking sheet, fill to the top. If you have leftover batter, fill little muffin cups for personal midnight snacks.

6. Place the brownies onto the oven's middle rack and bake for 30 to 35 minutes. Test doneness by inserting a toothpick and checking to see if it comes out clean. Store at room temperature for up to 2 days. They can be refrigerated for 1 week or frozen for 1 month.

RASTA MIXED BERRY SMOOTHIE

For something sweet, but also healthy, try this berry smoothie. Blueberries are the superfood show-offs, while raspberries have ellagic acid, which is known to have anti-cancer properties. Strawberries contain loads of heart-healthy vitamin C. Blackberries, though tart, can boost the sweetness profile of your smoothie while pulling a double to support oral and brain health. With some coconut-infused weed oil, you really can't get any better than this. Feel free to get creative with your smoothie by adding extras of your choice like chia seeds or hemp protein.

Time: 5 minutes 🍁 *Potency per serving:* 7.5 mg 🍁 *Yield:* 2 servings

WHAT YOU'LL NEED
1 cup coconut milk, water, or orange juice

1 teaspoon room-temperature cannabis-infused coconut oil

1 cup frozen berries of choice

WHAT TO DO
Add the liquid to a blender and start to pulse. Slowly add the coconut oil, then the frozen berries. Enjoy immediately.

I don't buy frozen berries, I actually buy them fresh from the *tianguis* (the native Mexican word for outdoor market). I eat some for a few days, then, before they get all weird and mushy and start to mold, I pop them in the freezer. Sometimes I cut up other fruits and put them all in there together to pull out and make a quick smoothie. It's been a game changer.

CRUNCHY CANNA COBBLER

Cobbler makes me feel cozy, fed, loved, hugged. I know it's a lot to expect from food, but let's just say I don't need a boyfriend or a lover—I need cobbler. I like mine extra crunchy so that when it's topped with ice cream or whipped cream, the mix with the crunch is blissful oblivion. Some like to add steel-cut oatmeal into their crust, and you can too. You can do whatever you want, and if that's having a relationship with cobbler, that's okay too.

Time: 1 hour ✸ *Potency per serving:* 4.8 mg ✸ *Yield:* 12 servings

WHAT YOU'LL NEED

6 tart apples, peeled, cored, and sliced

1½ cups brown sugar, divided

1 teaspoon ground cinnamon

2 cups flour

2 teaspoons baking powder

2 eggs

1 stick butter, melted

4 teaspoons cannabutter, melted

salt, to taste

1 scoop ice cream or whipped cream, optional

WHAT TO DO

1. Preheat the oven to 350°F.

2. In a large mixing bowl, mix the apples, ½ cup of brown sugar, pinch of salt, and cinnamon with a wooden spoon until all apples are evenly coated. In another bowl, add flour, pinch of salt, baking powder, the remaining sugar, eggs, and melted butters until the mixture is moist yet thick and even.

3. Grease a glass baking dish. Layer with apples, then cover evenly with the crust. Sometimes I like to layer a few slices of apples on the top.

4. Bake for 45 minutes or until crispy and brown. Serve hot with scoop of ice cream or dollop of whipped cream.

EASY BANANA BREAD MUFFINS

If I'm ever grabbing a cup of coffee from a local shop, I tend to treat myself to one of those little banana bread muffins. I'm usually really hungry and just not really prepared for the day and need a snack before any hanger erupts. They're so moist and you truly can't go wrong with banana bread. That's what these little muffins are to me, laced with some weed butter for extra chill vibes. Make enough for an entire week, or to share with your cranky coworkers.

Time: 40 minutes 🍁 *Potency:* 4.8 mg per muffin 🍁 *Yield:* 12 servings

WHAT YOU'LL NEED
3 very ripe bananas

2 eggs

2 cups flour

½ cup brown sugar

½ teaspoon salt

½ teaspoon baking soda

¼ cup pecans

4 teaspoons cannabutter

WHAT TO DO
1. Preheat the oven to 350°F.

2. Mash the bananas until soft and somewhat even in consistency, and whisk in eggs.

3. Gently mix in the flour, brown sugar, salt, baking soda, and pecans until fully incorporated.

4. Grease a 12-muffin tin, then pour in the batter. Bake muffins for 30 minutes and cool for 5 to 10 minutes before serving.

CONVERSION CHARTS

Volume

U.S.	U.S. Equivalent	Metric
1 tablespoon (3 teaspoons)	½ fluid ounce	15 milliliters
¼ cup	2 fluid ounces	60 milliliters
⅓ cup	3 fluid ounces	90 milliliters
½ cup	4 fluid ounces	120 milliliters
⅔ cup	5 fluid ounces	150 milliliters
¾ cup	6 fluid ounces	180 milliliters
1 cup	8 fluid ounces	240 milliliters
2 cups	16 fluid ounces	480 milliliters

Weight

U.S.	Metric
½ ounce	15 grams
1 ounce	30 grams
2 ounces	60 grams
¼ pound	115 grams
⅓ pound	150 grams
½ pound	225 grams
¾ pound	350 grams
1 pound	450 grams

Temperature

Fahrenheit (°F)	Celsius (°C)	Fahrenheit (°F)	Celsius (°C)
70°F	20°C	220°F	105°C
100°F	40°C	240°F	115°C
120°F	50°C	260°F	125°C
130°F	55°C	280°F	140°C
140°F	60°C	300°F	150°C
150°F	65°C	325°F	165°C
160°F	70°C	350°F	175°C
170°F	75°C	375°F	190°C
180°F	80°C	400°F	200°C
190°F	90°C	425°F	220°C
200°F	95°C	450°F	230°C

ACKNOWLEDGMENTS

I'm incredibly humbled by the support from all of my friends and family. Many thanks to Casie Vogel for taking a chance on me, and to Ellen Freeman for sparking the manifestation of a legit writing career in cannabis. To Maya Elisabeth, for bridging the gap between herb and my freelance career and all the opportunities and ancient cannabis knowledge you've passed on to me. To Karilily, the original connect who encouraged me to move to Humboldt County to start a new life. Thank you, James Oseland, for being my lightweight mentor. To Xiomara, Joy, and all of my sisters from another mister who've been in the weed game from day one and continue to carve an authentic future for women in weed. Thank you, David Lida, for your unwavering support and love. To my little sisters, Dinee and Lloa, and my stepmother, Geraldine, for keeping me connected to my West African roots. To my big brother, Fred, and my niece, Gabby. A special thanks to Cathy and Shannon for your generosity. To Sandra, my Virgo sis, and Jake, for your photography. A huge shout out to Anja and the entire Broccoli Mag crew for your support. Last but not least, thank you to those reading this: may you have a lifetime of health from cannabis.

ABOUT THE AUTHOR

Mennlay Golokeh Aggrey is an interdisciplinary cannabis entrepreneur and has been legally working with marijuana since 2005. As a creative in the field, she's worked for clients including Whoopi Goldberg and Maya Elisabeth for their Whoopi and Maya cannabis product line, and the award-winning pioneer edibles company, Om Edibles. She holds a B.A. in journalism and has worked professionally as a content creator and cannabis cultivator. She currently resides in Mexico City, Mexico, and Northern California as a freelance writer, researcher, and activist exploring cannabis, and the African diaspora in Latin America.